From Zero to Heat Pump Hero

Maximise Comfort and Efficiency: Your Guide to Understanding Your Air Source Heat Pump

Disclaimer
This book is intended to provide general information about air source heat pumps for homeowners. The information presented is based on the author's personal experiences and research, and does not constitute professional advice. Every property, heat pump unit and installation is unique. The recommendations and specifications provided by your installer and manufacturer should always be your primary reference for your specific heat pump system. The author and publisher cannot be held liable for any outcomes or issues that may arise from your heat pump installation or decisions made based on the information presented in this book.

Renewable Heating Hub
Join the heat pump conversation at Renewable Heating Hub, a helpful and approachable community for homeowners interested in renewable heating and heat pumps. Share your experiences, ask questions and connect with others passionate about sustainable living. Visit the Renewable Heating Hub forums to become part of this growing community:
https://renewableheatinghub.co.uk/forums

© Mars Mlodzinski 2024

Contents

Foreword 5
Welcome to the World of Heat Pumps 7
How Do Heat Pumps Work? 9
Control Panel: Understanding the Basics 13
Domestic Hot Water 17
Weather Compensation 23
Coefficient of Performance 25
Defrost Cycles 29
Monitoring & Optimising Performance 31
Open Loop Systems vs. Buffer Tanks 35
Flow Errors 39
Balancing Radiators 41
Index Circuit 43
Low Temperature System Design 45
Is Your Heat Pump Undersized? 49
Is Your Heat Pump Oversized? 53
Antifreeze Valves vs. Glycol 55
Insulation, Comfort & Efficiency 57
Regular Maintenance Schedule 61
Home & Emergency Insurance 65
Troubleshooting & Error Codes 67
Peace & Quiet 71
When to Call a Professional 73
Manufacturer Support 75
Heat Pumps, PV & Battery Storage 79
Electricity Tariffs 81
Lodging an Installation Complaint 83
Glossary 85
Units of Measurement 91

Foreword

Welcome to this guide on air source heat pumps (ASHPs), a technology at the forefront of our transition to a more sustainable, energy-efficient future. As the Head of Domestic Heat Pump Design at Net Zero, British Gas, I am delighted to see such an informative resource aimed at empowering homeowners to make the most of their heat pump systems.

Heat pumps are not merely a technological advancement – they are a crucial component of our journey towards net-zero carbon emissions. By harnessing free renewable energy from the air, heat pumps significantly reduce reliance on fossil fuels, thereby decreasing greenhouse gas emissions and contributing to a cleaner environment. However, the true potential of heat pumps can only be realised through meticulous system design, correct operation and robust support structures. When installing a heat pump, the way a house is heated changes, and this must be embraced by the homeowner for success. The system changes from a micromanaged, timed, zoned fossil fuel system to a continuously heated, comfortable environment.

The design of a heat pump system is paramount. A well-designed system ensures optimal performance, maximises energy efficiency, and guarantees comfort in your home throughout the year. For years, I have been emphasising the importance of tailoring each heat pump installation to the specific needs of the household, taking into account factors such as property size, insulation levels and individual heating requirements. Thoughtful design not only enhances efficiency and comfort levels but also prolongs the lifespan of the system, providing homeowners with reliable and cost-effective heating solutions.

However, even the most expertly designed systems require ongoing support and maintenance to function at their best. After installation, support is critical to addressing any teething problems, optimising system settings and ensuring homeowners are confident in operating their new systems.

Unfortunately, we have observed that support quality from installer to installer can vary significantly. It is imperative that manufacturers and installers alike commit to providing comprehensive aftercare, from troubleshooting guides to responsive customer service. Such support not only alleviates potential frustrations but also ensures the system's longevity and efficiency.

Homeowners' needs do not end once the installation is complete; they evolve as they familiarise themselves with their new heating system. Continuous education and support are essential in this regard. Providing homeowners with the resources to understand and manage their heat pumps effectively leads to better performance and greater satisfaction.

Brendon Uys
Head of Domestic Heat Pump Design, Net Zero British Gas

Welcome to the World of Heat Pumps

Congratulations on installing an air source heat pump! You've embraced a technology that represents a significant leap forward in energy efficiency and environmental responsibility, surpassing traditional heating methods like oil or gas boilers.

While the technology behind heat pumps may seem futuristic and innovative, its roots stretch back further than you might think. The conceptual foundation was laid in 1852 by Lord Kelvin, and the first practical application of heat recovery for domestic hot water emerged in the late 1940s thanks to Robert C. Webber's experimentation with his deep freezer. This innovation paved the way for modern heat pump systems. However, it wasn't until the 1970s that Dr. James Bose of Oklahoma State University truly propelled the technology forward, leading to significant advancements and establishing Oklahoma as a centre for heat pump research and development.

So, what sets air source heat pumps apart? Unlike traditional boilers that generate heat by burning fossil fuels, they operate on a fundamentally different principle. ASHPs efficiently extract heat from the outside air - even in cold conditions - and transfer it inside your home for heating and hot water. This process is highly efficient because it leverages ambient energy instead of relying on fossil fuel combustion.

Transitioning to a new heat pump heating system can be accompanied by questions and uncertainties because the fundamentals are so much different to fossil fuel boilers. Many homeowners initially find heat pumps challenging to understand and operate effectively, and are often left without adequate support or guidance from their installers.

Compounding this issue, user manuals tend to be overly technical and not very user-friendly, leaving homeowners feeling lost and frustrated. Without accessible resources or reliable help, many are left to fend for themselves. This book aims to bridge that gap and is

designed to be your guide, offering essential information, practical advice and instructions to help you maximise the efficiency and comfort of your new heating system and get tips on how to:
- Operate your air source heat pump more effectively
- Avoid common pitfalls
- Understand your system's control panel to adjust settings for optimal comfort and efficiency
- Maximise energy savings and optimise performance year-round
- Identify and troubleshoot common problems
- Develop routines to ensure your system's longevity and performance

By choosing an air source heat pump, you've opted for a more efficient, cost-effective heating solution and have made a meaningful contribution to reducing your carbon footprint and enhancing environmental sustainability. Our goal is to empower you to fully benefit from your heat pump, getting as much from it as possible, ensuring your home is comfortable, energy-efficient and environmentally friendly.

How Do Heat Pumps Work?

A heat pump is a system designed for the efficient transfer of heat from one place to another, essentially functioning as a conduit for energy. Think of a heat pump as a heat mover, not a heat generator.

Just like a household extractor fan moves warm air out of your kitchen, a heat pump moves heat from one place to another, but it takes it a step further, making the process more complex and efficient. Through the use of specialised fluids, conventional heat pumps can enhance the transferred heat to levels of energy that are practical for use, capable of reaching temperatures up to 55°C.

In the UK, air source heat pumps are prevalently installed due to their effectiveness and simplicity. These systems employ a robust fan that pulls air over a heat exchanger, effectively harvesting warmth from the air. This captured warmth is then transformed into energy, commonly used for heating water in radiator and underfloor heating circuits.

Ground source heat pumps operate in a similar manner by circulating a liquid through a network of underground pipes towards a heat exchanger, where the ground's natural warmth is absorbed and then converted into energy suitable for heating spaces or water supply. This book will focus primarily on the workings and benefits of air source heat pumps.

The Heat Pump Cycle

An ASHP works in a continuous cycle, constantly moving heat from one place to another. Here are the key parts involved:
- Evaporator: This component acts like a 'magnet' for heat. Air drawn in by the fan passes over a large, finned heat exchanger filled with refrigerant. As the air warms the refrigerant, it evaporates, absorbing heat in the process.

- Compressor: The refrigerant, now a gas, travels to the compressor. This device acts like a *pump*, squeezing the refrigerant gas, which significantly increases its temperature.
- Condenser: The hot, high-pressure gas then moves to the condenser. Here, it releases its heat to another fluid circulating through the heat exchanger. This heat can then be used to warm your home or hot water.
- Back to the Beginning: Once the refrigerant releases its heat, it cools down and condenses back into a liquid. It then travels back to the evaporator, ready to pick up more heat and start the cycle all over again.

Understanding the "Pump" in Your Heat Pump

Air source heat pumps might seem deceptively named with the term "pump" - after all, they aren't literally pushing (pumping) heat around like a water pump moves fluids. Instead, the "pumping" refers to their ability to move existing heat from one place to another, concentrating it in the process. This elevates the level of existing heat, making it usable for keeping your home warm and comfortable.

Refrigerant Cycle: Where the Magic Happens

To grasp how heat pumps generate heat through the refrigeration cycle, it's crucial to understand the relationship between pressure and temperature for a substance, in this case, refrigerant. Refrigerants are special fluids that have a very low boiling point. This means they can easily change from liquid to gas (and back again) at relatively low temperatures and pressures.

Let's use water as a relatable example: at sea level, water freezes at 0°C and boils at 100°C under atmospheric pressure. If the pressure increases, water requires more energy to change from a liquid to a gas, meaning its boiling point rises. For instance, at 1 bar above atmospheric pressure, water boils at around 120°C, and at 3 bar, it boils at approximately 144°C.

It's also vital to know that turning water from liquid to gas absorbs significantly more energy than simply heating it in its liquid form. For example, converting water to steam at 100°C consumes about five times more energy than heating water from 0°C to 100°C. This process stores a considerable amount of energy in the steam, which is released when the steam condenses back into water.

In the refrigeration cycle, this principle is harnessed to transfer heat. The cycle captures low-grade heat from sources like the air and transfers it, at a higher temperature, to a heating or hot water system. This is achieved by exploiting the energy changes during the refrigerant's phase transitions - first from liquid to gas, absorbing heat, and then from gas back to liquid, releasing heat.

The key to elevating the temperature of the collected low-grade heat to a useful level (around 50°C) is compression. By compressing the gaseous refrigerant, we increase its pressure and, consequently, its temperature. This compression is typically achieved with a compressor.

However, the efficiency of this process depends on how much the refrigerant can be compressed, which is limited by the capabilities of the compressor and the characteristics of the refrigerant.

A critical consideration is that higher compression - and therefore higher temperatures - requires more electrical energy. This interplay between energy input and temperature gain is a fundamental aspect of heat pump design and crucial for determining the efficiency of the system in heating applications.

Difference Between Temperature & Heat

Finally, when discussing heat pumps, it's important to also distinguish between temperature and heat. Heat refers to energy transfer, not how hot or cold something feels. For example, imagine a large, open-sided tent in a cold environment. If only a few people enter and start dancing, the tent's temperature stays about the same as the outside. But if the tent fills with more dancers, each emitting about a hundred watts of heat, the collective energy significantly warms the tent, despite its open sides.

This analogy applies to how heat pumps work in buildings. Heat pumps function effectively by transferring energy into a space at a rate that exceeds energy loss. The goal is to continuously push heat into the building to maintain a comfortable indoor temperature, even when it's cold outside.

With this in mind, heat pump efficiency can be further optimised by using a wet central heating system, like radiators or underfloor heating, with water circulating at a lower temperature. This approach improves heat transfer because cooler water allows the heat pump to operate at a lower temperature difference between the heat source (outside air) and the heat delivery system (water). This smaller temperature gap translates to less work for the compressor, which significantly reduces its electricity consumption. It's a great example of how thoughtful system design directly impacts the effectiveness of heat pumps in maintaining comfortable indoor temperatures while minimising energy use. We'll circle back to explore this later in the book, but first, let's focus on your heat pump's controller.

Control Panel: Understanding the Basics

Mastering your heat pump's control panel puts you in charge of comfort, efficiency and running costs. It's the central hub for managing your heating and hot water settings, allowing you to customise temperatures, set schedules and even monitor energy usage. By understanding the different functions and features of your control panel, you'll gain the ability to fine-tune your heat pump's operation, ensuring your home is always comfortable while minimising energy waste.

Control panels typically consists of a display screen and buttons. While specific layouts, options and features you can access may vary between brands and models, most control panels share core functionalities. When you access your heat pump's control panel, the display screen usually showcases vital information about its operation. Key elements might include:

- Current room temperature: Displays the real-time temperature of the area connected to the heat pump's thermostat.
- Set point flow temperature: This reflects the desired temperature you've programmed the system to maintain. If this is enabled, you should consider switching this mode to weather compensation.
- Operating mode: This indicates the current mode your ASHP is functioning in - heating, hot water, defrost, standby, off, etc.
- Domestic hot water temperature: This displays the current temperature of your hot water storage tank.
- Energy Monitoring: Some control panels display real-time energy usage and might even include historical consumption data, allowing you to track your heat pump's efficiency and easily calculate your COP.
- Diagnostic Information: Some systems may offer more in-depth technical readouts for parameters like pressure, flow rate or

refrigerant temperatures. This can be helpful for troubleshooting or for those who like to monitor their system closely.
- Outdoor temperature: This displays the current outside temperature.
- Holiday Mode: This setting maintains a lower base temperature while you're away, saving energy without letting your home get too cold.
- Timer Functions: Many control panels let you programme heating and hot water schedules, customising these for different times and days of the week.
- Error codes: In case of any malfunctions, the display might indicate error codes for troubleshooting.

Here's a breakdown of some essential controls you'll likely encounter on your ASHP control panel:
- Power Button: This turns the entire system on or off.
- Mode Button: This allows you to switch between different operating modes (set point flow temperature, weather compensation, standby, etc.).
- Temperature: Increase or decrease the desired temperature setting for your central heating.
- Hot Water Controls: Separate temperature settings for your hot water, or a dedicated button to activate hot water boost.
- Connectivity: If the control panel offers smart home features, you may see buttons or menus related to WiFi setup or linking to an app.
- Clock: For scheduling features to work, your heat pump may have a built-in clock that you can set.
- Menu Button: This might access more advanced settings and functionalities.
- Back Button: This navigates back from menus or settings adjustments.

Many control panels use symbols and icons to represent different functions. To fully understand what each symbol means on your specific model, it's essential to consult your user manual or search for it online. Every heat pump brand designs its control panel slightly differently, so your user manual is an invaluable resource. It provides detailed instructions specific to your model, explaining the control panel functionalities, troubleshooting steps and essential maintenance procedures. Carefully reviewing the manual will ensure you fully understand the capabilities of your ASHP and operate it effectively.

It's important to note that some sections of your control panel might be password-protected and "hidden" from general access. These sections typically house advanced settings related to installation, servicing, commissioning and maintenance. Accessing these settings is generally reserved for qualified installers or technicians to prevent accidental changes that could impact the system's performance or safety. If you require assistance with advanced settings or suspect an issue with your ASHP, don't hesitate to contact your installer, a certified technician or even your manufacturer. However, as you become more familiar with how your heat pump works, gaining access to this section might allow you to tweak your settings further, unlocking even greater efficiency from your system.

Additional Tips
- Familiarise yourself with the control panel layout and basic functions before making adjustments.
- Know how to turn the heat pump on and off.
- Start with simple adjustments like changing the set point temperature and exploring different operating modes like weather compensation.
- Refer to the user manual for detailed instructions and advanced features.
- Don't hesitate to contact your installer or a qualified technician if you encounter any issues or require further assistance.
- If you're still struggling and can't find what you're looking for on your control panel, you can always visit the forums at Renewable Heating Hub - https://renewableheatinghub.co.uk/forums - and other homeowners with the same brand and model of heat pump will probably be able to assist and point you in the right direction.

Make Your Own Notes Here:

Domestic Hot Water

Harnessing the full potential of your heat pump for domestic hot water is essential for achieving both comfort and energy efficiency. When correctly installed and configured, your heat pump provides a reliable supply of hot water while significantly reducing energy consumption. By understanding and making a few key adjustments, you can optimise its performance, ensuring a steady flow of hot water and lower energy bills.

Hot Water Production Modes

Many heat pumps prioritise hot water production over space heating, a feature that maximises efficiency. This is especially valuable during the warmer months when you don't need central heating but still require a steady supply of hot water for daily needs like showers, baths and washing up.

Understanding Efficiency

While ASHPs excel at generating hot water for your home, maximising their efficiency is key to enjoying their benefits without excessive energy costs. Low-temperature heat pumps, currently the most common type in the UK, operate at peak efficiency when generating hot water at around 45°C. Pushing them to produce hotter water decreases efficiency, leading to higher energy bills. Additionally, overheating hot water creates unnecessary energy waste and significantly increases the risk of dangerous scalding incidents.

Legionnaires' Disease Prevention

Your heat pump likely includes a vital safety feature called a Legionnaires' cycle. Legionnaires' disease is a potentially severe form of pneumonia caused by bacteria that can thrive in warm, stagnant water. While a comfortable hot water temperature is important, it's essential to prevent this bacterial growth. That's where the Legionnaires' cycle comes in. Your ASHP may periodically boost your hot water tank temperature to 60°C, effectively sterilising the water and eliminating any harmful bacteria, ensuring the safety of your hot water supply.

In most cases, Legionnaires' cycles are made possible by an immersion heater - a backup electric heating element within your hot water cylinder. While immersion heaters are a reliable way to achieve the high temperatures needed for sterilisation, there's a downside: they can be significantly more energy-intensive and expensive to operate than the heat pump itself. This is particularly true if you have a large hot water cylinder. It's important to balance the need for safety with the potential increase in energy costs when these cycles occur.

Maximising Efficiency

Here's how you can optimise your hot water production with your air source heat pump:
- Set the hot water temperature: Most ASHP control panels allow you to adjust the desired hot water temperature. Aim for a setting around 44-45°C for optimal efficiency and to avoid scalding risks.
- Schedule Hot Water Heating: If your ASHP control panel offers scheduling options, consider programming hot water heating during off-peak hours when electricity rates might be lower, especially if you are on a time of use tariff with your electricity provider..
- Minimise Hot Water Usage: Simple practices like shorter showers and using water-efficient appliances can significantly reduce hot water demand and energy consumption.
- Differential: When heating water with a heat pump, it's most efficient to aim for longer heating sessions rather than quick bursts. In our experience, setting the water temperature to 45°C works well, but we also learned that adjusting the temperature differential setting significantly enhances efficiency. By default, our heat pump was set with a 5°C differential. This meant that if our hot water target was 45°C and the tank temperature dropped to 39.9°C, the heat pump would activate and work to quickly bring the temperature back up to 45°C. This frequent, high-speed operation isn't the most efficient mode for a heat pump. After experimentation and considering that most hot water cylinders are stratified (layered with

different water temperatures), we discovered an interesting detail. Even when our control panel indicated that the tank temperature had dropped to 28°C, the water from the tap was still around 45°C. So we decided to adjust our differential setting from 5°C to 15°C. With this wider temperature differential, the heat pump now operates over a longer period to gently reheat the water. This adjustment proved far more efficient. For instance, our heat pump, with a Seasonal Coefficient of Performance (SCOP) of 2.7, was able to generate 8 kWh of heat using just 2.75 kWh of electricity, achieving a COP of 2.90 to reheat our hot water. This method of reheating hot water, with less frequent but longer sessions, turned out to be much more efficient than the quick, short bursts we were initially set up to do. You might find a similar setting under a different name on your heat pump's control panel, but adjusting it could significantly improve your system's efficiency.

Consulting Your User Manual

For specifics on your ASHP's hot water production capabilities, Legionnaires' cycle details and any available scheduling options, refer to your user manual if you can't locate them in the control panel settings.

Monitor Your Heating in the Summer

Homeowners should be vigilant about their domestic hot water heating during the summer months when their heating is off. On the Renewable Heating Hub forums, numerous cases have been reported where, due to poor installation, inadequate design, and insufficient controls, systems intended to heat only water for domestic use still activate distribution pumps that circulate hot water to heating circuits. We've even seen cases where hot water has 'leaked' into the heating circuits after Legionnaires' cycles, heating radiators and underfloor heating, pointing to diverter valves that have not been correctly installed. These faults not only waste energy but also increase utility costs unnecessarily. It's essential for homeowners to regularly monitor their systems and, if they notice this problem, to call a qualified installer to inspect and rectify the system to ensure it operates efficiently and as intended.

Solar Diverters, ASHPs & Hot Water

Solar diverters are devices designed to optimise the use of excess energy generated by solar PV panels. Traditionally, when solar panels produce more electricity than a household can immediately use, this surplus energy is sent back to the grid. A solar diverter can redirect this excess electricity to heat water via an immersion heater in the cylinder. While this might seem like a seamless integration of renewable technologies, the application may not always be the most efficient or necessary, especially in homes equipped with heat pumps. That's because air source heat pumps are efficient systems that can heat water using significantly less electrical energy compared to traditional heating methods, including those using diverters with standard immersion heaters.

The efficiency of ASHPs is measured by their COP (which we'll cover in a future chapter), which quantifies how effectively a heat pump converts electrical energy into heat energy. This is where the distinction between the two systems becomes important for homeowners considering their energy setups.

We put it to the test in our home and conducted an experiment to directly compare the efficiency of a solar diverter with our air source heat pump in heating a 300-litre hot water tank to 45°C. This test was designed to determine which method would be more electricity-efficient and whether it justifies using a solar diverter in a home already equipped with an ASHP.

Using the heat pump we used approximately 5.81 kWh of electricity to reheat our hot water when the tank temperature dropped under 30°C. This calculation is based on our heat pump's COP of 2.7. If your heat pump has a higher COP if will be even more efficient at heating the hot water.

Using the immersion heater alone (powered directly by the PV system) required 15.70 kWh of electricity to reheat the hot water to 45°C after it had dropped below 30°C. Using our heat pump to heat our hot water is a significantly more efficient decision - a whole 2.7 times more efficient than relying on the solar diverter and immersion heater.

This efficiency difference forces us to think carefully about how we use our solar energy. While directly using solar power for hot water via an immersion heater seems like the ultimate in sustainability, sometimes a slightly less direct approach is ultimately better for the planet. Because the heat pump is so efficient, it still utilises the energy from your solar panels, but with less total electricity required. This allows you to export surplus electricity to the grid, reducing reliance on fossil-fuel power plants and maximising the benefits of your renewable energy system across your whole community.

Make Your Own Notes Here:

Weather Compensation

Weather compensation is a key feature for optimising the performance and cost-effectiveness of air source heat pumps. Imagine a traditional heating system as a chef who always cooks at the same high temperature, regardless of the dish. This inflexible approach often leads to energy waste and uneven heating.

In contrast, weather compensation allows your heat pump to act as an intelligent chef, continuously monitoring the outside temperature and adjusting the heat output accordingly. This ensures your home maintains a consistently comfortable temperature while minimising energy consumption. By adapting to real-time weather conditions, weather compensation helps you achieve a more efficient heating system, resulting in lower energy bills and enhanced comfort.

Efficiency Through Precision

Here's how weather compensation translates into real-world benefits:

- Reduced Energy Consumption: During mild weather, your ASHP doesn't need to work as hard to maintain warmth inside your home. Weather compensation automatically adjusts the flow temperature to a lower level, requiring less energy to heat the water and deliver the desired comfort level.

- Improved System Lifespan: By operating at lower temperatures when possible, weather compensation reduces unnecessary wear and tear on your ASHP's components, potentially extending its lifespan.

- Enhanced Comfort: Weather compensation ensures a more consistent and comfortable heating experience throughout your home. Gone are the days of fluctuating temperatures, with chilly radiators on mild days or sweltering rooms during unexpected warm spells. This feature allows the system to automatically and precisely adjust its heat output to maintain your desired comfort level, regardless of changing outdoor temperatures.

Make Sure It's Turned On

Unfortunately, many installers often disable weather compensation on air source heat pump systems to avoid customer complaints. This is because, with weather compensation, your radiators won't get as scorching hot as they might with a traditional gas or oil boiler. However, this constant high-temperature operation sacrifices efficiency, leading to significantly higher heating bills, especially during mild spells.

The importance of activating weather compensation cannot be overstated. It's the key to maximising your heat pump's performance and unlocking serious energy savings. Weather compensation works in tandem with heat curves, which dictate how your system adjusts the flow temperature based on the outside temperature. Properly configured heat curves ensure your home remains comfortably warm without unnecessary energy consumption.

As a homeowner, it's worth being proactive. Finding the perfect heat curve for your home may require some trial and error, as each home is unique. Adjusting the settings incrementally and monitoring the results will help you identify the most efficient configuration.

Remember, even radiators that don't feel hot can still effectively heat your home when the system is running optimally. This simple adjustment can deliver both lower energy bills and a more comfortable living space with fewer temperature fluctuations. Be patient and persistent, and you will find the ideal settings to maximise your heat pump's efficiency.

Coefficient of Performance

For homeowners aiming to maximise their system's effectiveness, grasping the concept of COP (Coefficient of Performance) is essential. This critical metric reveals how efficiently your heat pump converts energy into heat, allowing you to make informed running decisions and optimise performance.

What is COP?

The COP is a measure that indicates how efficiently a heat pump uses electricity to move heat from one place to another. Specifically, it's the ratio of heat output (in kilowatts) to electrical energy input (also in kilowatts) over a specific period. In simpler terms, COP tells you how many units of heat your ASHP delivers for every unit of electricity it consumes.

A COP of 3, for instance, indicates that for every unit of electricity the pump uses, it generates three units of heat, translating to a remarkable 300% efficiency. This level of performance means that the system is three times more efficient than direct electric heating, where one unit of electrical energy produces one unit of heat. The higher the COP, the higher the efficiency.

However, it's important to note that a heat pump's COP isn't static; it can fluctuate based on several external factors. The outdoor temperature significantly influences the COP because heat pumps draw heat from the outside air, and the warmer the air, the less work the pump has to do to raise its temperature to a suitable level for heating your home. Conversely, as the outdoor temperature drops, the COP tends to decrease since the system must work harder.

Similarly, the temperature setting of the heating system also affects the COP. Setting the system to maintain a higher indoor temperature requires more energy, reducing the overall efficiency.

SCOP: The Bigger Picture
While COP gives you a snapshot of efficiency at a specific moment, it doesn't tell the whole story for year-round use. That's where SCOP (Seasonal Coefficient of Performance) comes in. SCOP calculates the average efficiency of your heat pump over an entire heating season (or the life of your system), taking into account the variations in temperature we experience. This provides a more realistic and comprehensive picture of how your heat pump actually performs throughout the year.

Why COP & SCOP Matters
Understanding your heat pumps' COP and SCOP is crucial for several reasons:
- Energy Efficiency: A higher COP (at a given moment) means lower energy bills and reduced environmental impact.
- System Performance: Tracking COP over time helps you spot potential performance issues. SCOP should stay reasonably consistent year-to-year, so a big change could indicate a need for an investigation because something may be wrong.
- Cost-Effectiveness: Knowing the COP and SCOP can help you make informed decisions about your heating needs, ensuring you're getting the most out of your investment.

Benchmarking
- Identify Your ASHP's COP: This information can typically be found in the product specifications or obtained from the manufacturer. Some systems display real-time COP data directly on their control panels. Comparing your real-time COP readings to these specifications can reveal if your system is underperforming in specific conditions.
- Monitor and Record: Regularly check the COP if your system allows. Keeping a record over different months and seasons (building a SCOP picture in the process) can provide valuable insights into how your ASHP performs under various conditions.
- Compare and Analyse: Use the recorded COP values to determine if there are significant fluctuations in efficiency under certain weather conditions and temperatures. A consistent drop may signal

that something has gone wrong and that maintenance or an adjustment is required.
• Don't Forget Comfort: While COP and SCOP are valuable measures of efficiency, remember that system design and sizing also play a significant role. A very efficient heat pump that's too small for your home might struggle to maintain comfortable temperatures, regardless of its impressive COP figures.
• Consult with Professionals: If you're unsure about your ASHP's performance or how to improve its COP, consulting with a qualified heat pump technician can provide you with tailored advice and solutions.

Tips for Optimising COP
• Weather Compensation: Weather compensation is the single most effective way to boost your COP. This feature allows the system to automatically adjust to changing weather conditions, maximising efficiency throughout the heating season. Experimenting with heat curves may also lead to better results.
• Insulation Matters: A well-insulated home is your heat pump's best friend. Reducing heat loss means less work for your heat pump, which can directly improve its COP while improving overall comfort too.
• Minimise Hot Water Boosts: If your heat pump has a hot water boost feature, use it sparingly. Boosting water temperature beyond the usual target can significantly reduce efficiency. Use our hot water tips provided earlier to improve your COP.
• Consider an Upgrade: If your heat pump is very old, a newer model will likely offer a significantly higher COP. While upgrading is an investment, the long-term energy savings can make it worthwhile.

Understanding and utilising the COP of your air source heat pump is more than just knowing a number - it's the key to unlocking the full potential of your home heating system. By actively tracking your COP (and using it to paint a SCOP picture), you gain valuable insights into how efficiently your heat pump is operating.

Make Your Own Notes Here:

Defrost Cycles

Have you ever noticed your air source heat pump releasing steam on a cold day? Don't worry; it's a normal process called the defrost cycle. During colder weather, moisture in the air can freeze on the outdoor coils of your heat pump, hindering its efficiency. To address this, heat pumps have a defrost cycle that removes frost or ice buildup from the outdoor coils.

Heat Extraction & Frost Build up

You already know that your heat pump extracts heat from the outside air, even on cold days. The outdoor unit contains a component called the evaporator coil, which functions as a heat exchanger. As air passes over this coil, heat energy is absorbed and transferred into your heating system. When temperatures typically drop below 3°C, especially in humid conditions, moisture in the air can condense and freeze on the evaporator coil. This accumulated frost acts as an insulating layer, reducing the heat pump's ability to effectively extract warmth from the outside air.

Melting the Frost

To combat the frost that forms on the evaporator coil during cold and humid conditions, your ASHP initiates a defrost cycle:

- The system temporarily reverses its operation. The outdoor unit becomes a temporary heater.
- Warm refrigerant is pumped through the evaporator coil. This melts the accumulated frost, which then exits the unit as water. Due to the temperature difference, this water may appear as steam.
- The defrost cycle requires more energy. You may notice a slight increase in your energy consumption during this time. However, this additional energy ensures efficient heat extraction in the long run.

Interestingly, this process uses a minimal amount of heat from the system. For example, a 12kW heat pump might only draw about 0.8 kW from the system water during defrosting. This could result in a temporary drop in system water temperature - say, from 40°C to 30°C over 5-10 minutes in a 70-litre system, a change typically unnoticed on most UK systems due to measures like on-off thermostats, buffer tanks and system separation, but these can also lead to more frequent defrost cycles.

Defrost cycles vary in duration, generally lasting a few minutes to efficiently remove frost. However, defrosting that extends beyond 10 minutes is uncommon and indicative of potential issues needing investigation. Homeowners should be aware that extended defrost times of over 30 minutes (which we have seen reports of on Renewable Heating Hub) are not standard and warrant a closer look.

Monitoring & Optimising Performance

To fully optimise your heat pump's capabilities, it's essential to delve deeper into its performance beyond just adjusting the temperature setting to your liking. Understanding various aspects such as efficiency, capacity utilisation and system dynamics plays a crucial role in maximising the potential of your heat pump. By gaining insights into these factors, you can ensure that your heat pump operates at its peak performance, delivering optimal comfort and efficiency for your home heating needs.

The Importance of Monitoring

While basic heat pump controls enable temperature adjustments and mode selection (such as setting the flow temperature or using weather compensation), real optimisation comes from monitoring your heat pump's performance and understanding it. This data provides valuable insights into energy consumption, system efficiency and potential issues, ultimately empowering you to:

- Optimise Settings: Analyse data to adjust operating parameters for different weather conditions, maximising efficiency and minimising energy consumption.

- Identify Potential Problems: Early detection of inefficiencies or malfunctions allows for timely intervention, preventing costly repairs and ensuring system longevity.

- Track Energy Usage: Monitor energy consumption over time to understand your heat pump's impact on your energy bills and identify opportunities for further savings.

- Making Informed Upgrades: Long-term data can be invaluable if you consider future system or home upgrades (such as adding more insulation). It provides a baseline to compare against to see if the upgrades made a measurable difference.

- Gain Peace of Mind: Real-time data provides reassurance about your system's performance, ensuring it operates efficiently and reliably, and not getting nasty surprises when your electricity bill arrives.

Levels of Monitoring

The extent of monitoring capabilities provided by your heat pump can vary considerably, ranging from basic to advanced levels of functionality and data access. Here's a breakdown of what you might encounter:

Basic Monitoring

Most ASHP controllers offer basic monitoring capabilities, typically displaying:
- Flow Temperatures: Some controllers show water temperatures entering and leaving the heat pump, providing a basic insight into the system's performance.
- Operating Status: Information about the current operating mode (heating, standby, domestic hot water) is usually displayed.
- Error Codes: Some controllers may display basic error codes, alerting you to potential malfunctions.

Additional Features (not common on many heat pumps)
- Energy Consumption: Some controllers might display the current energy consumption in kW or kWh, and also give you historic data over time (week, month, etc.). Some might even show the split between domestic hot water and central heating consumption.
- DHW and Central Heating Split: Some heat pumps allow you to see a split in electricity consumption between DHW and central heating, enabling you to assess the efficiency of each.

While this basic monitoring provides a general overview, which might be sufficient for most homeowners, it often lacks the detailed data needed for in-depth analysis and optimisation if you really want to get the most out of your system. For those seeking deeper insights, several options exist for gaining a more thorough understanding:

Third-party Monitoring Systems

These systems connect directly to your heat pump, providing comprehensive data through dedicated apps or online dashboards. They often offer features like:

- Real-time data: Monitor live data points like energy consumption, water flow rates, COP and individual sensor readings.
- Historical Data Analysis: Track performance trends over time, identify patterns, and assess the impact of adjustments made at different times of the year. Data can then be exported as graphs for easy comparison.
- Performance Benchmarking: Compare your ASHP's performance against similar systems in your area or industry standards to gauge its efficiency and identify areas for improvement.
- Alerts and notifications: Receive alerts for potential issues, abnormal operating conditions or maintenance reminders.
- Remote control: Adjust settings and operating modes remotely, even when you're away from home.
- Integration with Smart Home Systems: Seamlessly integrate monitoring data with other smart home devices or systems, enabling automation and optimisation of energy usage. This trend is expected to grow, with features such as weather station integration and weather predictions enhancing system efficiency even further.

Open-source Monitoring Solutions

Creative and tech-savvy heat pump users can take their monitoring to the next level with open-source platforms and compatible hardware. These systems offer unparalleled flexibility and customisation. Users can tailor their data collection, create their own unique dashboards, and even set up sophisticated automations based on their heat pump's performance.

While this approach requires more technical knowledge and potentially some hardware investment, the results can be incredibly powerful. If you have the DIY spirit and want to truly understand the inner workings of your system, explore the amazing examples of user-created monitoring setups on the Renewable Heating Hub forums: https://renewableheatinghub.co.uk/forums.

Choosing the Right Monitoring Solution

The ideal monitoring solution depends on your specific needs and technical capabilities. Consider the following factors:

- Desired level of data: Determine the specific data points you want to monitor for optimal analysis and optimisation.
- Technical expertise: Some solutions require technical knowledge for installation and configuration.
- Cost: Third-party monitoring systems often involve subscription fees, while open-source solutions may require upfront hardware investments.
- Compatibility: Some monitoring systems are only compatible with specific heat pump brands and models. If you have a less well-known or less commonly installed brand of heat pump, your options may be limited.
- Cloud vs. Local Data Storage: Some homeowners prefer local storage of data only, as they may have concerns about downtime, connectivity issues and security risks associated with cloud-based solutions. Local storage provides more control over data privacy and security, but may require additional hardware and maintenance.

Open Loop Systems vs. Buffer Tanks

The design of a heating system has a profound impact on the lifespan of a heat pump. Similar to any machine, frequent on-and-off cycles, known as short cycling, can significantly reduce its operational life. For example, a well-maintained truck engine, which undergoes long intervals between starts, can easily exceed 1,000,000 miles. In contrast, a Formula 1 engine, subject to constant high performance and frequent cycling, only lasts a few thousand miles.

In heat pumps, if the system cycles frequently, running at peak power and high temperatures for short periods, its lifespan will be shortened. Conversely, allowing the heat pump to modulate continually at lower temperatures can extend its lifespan significantly.

In the UK, heat pump installers often default to using buffer tanks, system separators and volumisers to smooth out flow rates and maintain system volume. However, the belief that buffer tanks effectively smooth out load is a growing misconception. For instance, a 100-litre buffer holds only 1.17 kW of energy at a temperature 10°C higher than required. If the system's load is 10 kW, this translates to about 7 minutes of buffer time, which is not significant. Furthermore, achieving that extra 10°C in temperature can increase energy bills by up to 25%.

Using on-off thermostats and buffer tanks generally causes cycling and forces the heat pump to run at peak power and high temperatures to heat the house. In contrast, an open zone, whole-house operation allows the heat pump to operate for longer durations at lower temperatures, promoting a longer lifespan and greater efficiency.

The Case for Open Loop Systems

Unlike closed-loop systems, where your heat pump heats a closed circuit of water that then exchanges heat with your heat emitters, open-loop systems directly use the water heated by the heat pump throughout your entire home. This offers a distinct advantage: the potential for simpler, more efficient temperature control. With an open-loop system, you can adjust the temperature for your entire house at once, eliminating the need to manage individual TRVs in each room.

Understanding On-Off Thermostats in Heating Systems

On-off thermostats or other controls do not directly modulate the output of the heating plant, leading to inefficiencies in the system operation. When an on-off thermostat signals that the room, underfloor heating or house temperature is satisfied, the entire system typically switches off, including the heat pump.

For example, a 5 kW heat pump designed with a duty point flow temperature of 45°C for radiator heating would have a system volume of approximately 60 litres. At around 50% load, which corresponds to a temperature of approximately 5°C, the flow temperature would ideally be around 38°C with weather compensation.

When the thermostat signals to switch on, the water temperature will be close to the desired room temperature, typically around 20°C. This results in a Delta T of 18°C between the desired water temperature and room temperature.

To bring the water up to the desired temperature when the thermostat switches on, the heat pump will require approximately 15 minutes of full power operation before it begins to modulate, assuming it is on weather compensation control. However, if it is on direct water temperature control, the unit will continue to run at full capacity until the thermostat is satisfied. Running a heat pump at full capacity for extended periods leads to poor performance.

For optimal performance and temperature consistency in modulating heating systems, it's advisable to refrain from installing controls on common area emitters and only regulate temperatures in bedrooms. In cases where there's a risk of excessive thermal gain, partial control of those areas might be warranted.

Why Less is More

TRVs and room thermostats are designed to maintain a specific temperature in each room. However, for open loop ASHP systems, these individual controls can be counterproductive. Constant adjustments by thermostats and TRVs can lead to frequent on-and-off cycles for the ASHP, compromising efficiency.

Steady Flow

Open loop systems excel when operating with a single system-wide temperature control. This allows the heat pump to maintain a steady flow of warm water throughout the entire system. Instead of constantly reacting to individual room temperature fluctuations, the system focuses on maintaining a consistent overall temperature, minimising short cycling and maximising efficiency.

Balancing for Comfort

Ditching individual thermostatic radiator valves might seem like you're losing control over room-by-room temperatures. However, rebalancing your radiators can solve this. By carefully adjusting the flow rate to each radiator, a skilled heating professional can ensure even warmth throughout your home. This eliminates the need for individual TRVs and creates a comfortable living environment.

Rebalancing is especially beneficial for low-temperature systems like air source heat pumps, as it helps rooms reach their desired temperature more evenly and efficiently. You can even use this balancing technique to fine-tune the heat distribution between your radiators and underfloor heating.

Making the Switch

While this book focuses on getting the most out of your existing air source heat pump, it's valuable to be aware of potential future upgrades like open-loop systems. If you're planning major renovations, consider discussing this option with a qualified installer when the opportunity arises.

Transitioning from a closed-loop system with TRVs to a single-temperature open-loop setup requires professional expertise. A qualified heating engineer can evaluate your specific setup and recommend the best approach. They'll handle the necessary plumbing modifications and system rebalancing, which often involves removing or bypassing buffer tanks to optimise your heat pump's efficiency.

If your home has microbore piping (smaller diameter pipes), a buffer tank might still be necessary, and in many cases an existing buffer tank can often be modified to act as a volumiser. This modification can lead to performance and efficiency improvements for your heat pump system as a whole.

Embracing the Benefits

Simplifying your heat pump system by minimising stop-and-start cycles through a centralised control and potentially removing TRVs offers numerous advantages:
- Improved Efficiency: Less short cycling translates to significant energy savings and lower running costs.
- Enhanced System Lifespan: Reduced stress on the ASHP and compressor from frequent on-and-off cycles can potentially extend its lifespan.
- Quieter Operation: Fewer on-and-off cycles create a smoother and quieter heating experience.

Open Loop Potential

Adopting this approach may necessitate disruptive adjustments to your system, but the long-term rewards - enhanced energy efficiency, improved comfort and extended system lifespan - can be substantial. Many UK installers have yet to adopt this method, often applying traditional boiler management techniques to air source heat pumps. Consulting with a qualified professional is crucial to assess whether transitioning your system to an open loop with a single control strategy could maximise your ASHP's performance. If finding an experienced installer poses a challenge, consider seeking advice and recommendations on the Renewable Heating Hub forums at https://renewableheatinghub.co.uk/forums.

Flow Errors

While encountering an error message like "flow error" or a cryptic code on your heat pump's control panel can be unsettling, it's important to remember that these specific occurrences don't necessarily signal a major malfunction. These error codes often indicate temporary issues with water flow within the system, which can have various causes.

The Y Strainer and Other Filters

In many air-to-water heat pump systems, a crucial but often overlooked component is the Y strainer (also called a gauze filter). Situated along the water line entering your heat pump, it performs the vital task of filtering out debris. This strainer acts like a bodyguard, protecting your heat pump from dirt, rust, gunk and other contaminants.

The Blockage

Over time, with all the water that passes through it, the Y strainer can become clogged. This is especially likely if you have older pipes or if any work has been done on your system recently that might have introduced debris. If you have additional filters within your system these can also clog. When this happens, water can't flow freely to your heat pump, potentially triggering a "flow error". Remember, ASHPs need significantly more water flow than traditional fossil fuel boilers, so even a partial blockage can cause problems. If the flow issue is severe enough, the ASHP will shut down automatically as a self-preservation measure.

Preventing Flow Errors

Avoiding most flow errors involves straightforward maintenance - primarily, the regular cleaning of the Y strainer and/or any other installed filters. Most manufacturers advise cleaning the Y strainer at least once a year. It is also often advised to clean out the filter the week you turn your heating on for the first time ahead of the heating season.

Cleaning Steps:
- Turn off/isolate the water supply before and after the filter.
- Locate the Y strainer and unscrew the bottom cap.
- Remove any trapped debris, and clean the strainer mesh under running water.
- Reassemble, ensuring a tight seal.
- Turn the water supply to the ASHP back on.

Consult your heat pump's manual or ask a professional for detailed instructions tailored to your specific model and set up. You also might not have a Y strainer and you may have a different filter installed on your system. Follow the specific steps to clean that filter.

Looking Beyond the Filter

While the Y strainer plays a crucial role, other factors can also trigger flow errors, including:
- Blocked Pipes: Mineral buildup or debris accumulation can restrict water flow.
- Airlocks: Trapped air in the system may interrupt water flow, causing errors.
- Pump Issues: A malfunctioning circulation pump could lead to inadequate flow.

If cleaning the Y strainer or other filter doesn't solve the problem, a comprehensive check by a qualified heat pump engineer is advisable. They can inspect for blockages, airlocks and pump functionality to resolve your flow error.

By prioritising high flow rates and maintaining your heat pump's filters, you can prevent flow errors, ensuring your system operates smoothly, keeping your home warm and comfortable.

Balancing Radiators

While your heat pump and central heating system works to circulate hot water throughout your home, it's possible that not all rooms are experiencing the same level of comfort. Picture this: you're relaxing in the living room, enjoying cosy warmth, while your TV room remains stubbornly chilly. Or perhaps the upstairs feels like a sauna, while the downstairs struggles to shake off the winter chill.

With heat pumps, this uneven heat is not uncommon and often means your radiators are not balanced. Each radiator contributes to the warmth in your home, but sometimes they need adjusting to work together properly.

Consequences of Uneven Heat Distribution

- Uneven Room Temperatures: Some rooms become uncomfortably hot while others remain cool, leading to frustration and a less than ideal living environment.
- Wasted Energy: A system that isn't balanced forces your ASHP to work harder to compensate for temperature differences, resulting in higher energy bills and unnecessary wear and tear on your system.
- Reduced Comfort: Who wants to fight for comfort in their own home? Uneven temperatures lead to dreaded thermostat wars and a less comfortable living experience, which is deadly for a heat pump's performance.

Diagnosing the Imbalance

Before diving into balancing, identify the symptoms:
- Hot and Cold Rooms: The most obvious sign is a noticeable temperature difference between rooms with radiators.
- Lukewarm Radiators: If some radiators feel cool to the touch even when the flow temperature is set high, it might indicate insufficient hot water flow.

Balancing Your Way to Comfort

Most radiators have lockshield valves and thermostatic radiator valves (TRVs) with numbered settings. Smart TRVs display precise temperatures in Celsius or Fahrenheit depending on your preferences. Before making any adjustments, carefully review your radiator setup and the next chapter on the index circuit, which will help you confirm adequate pressure in your heating system.

Balancing radiators involves adjusting these valves to ensure each receives the right amount of hot water based on its size and position. This process creates consistent warmth throughout your home. Begin with the radiator closest to the heat pump on the heating circuit. Slowly open its lockshield valve until the desired temperature is reached, then move on to the next radiator.

For TRVs, if you don't have an open-loop system, setting them to the highest level allows maximum water and heat into the radiator. With smart TRVs, increase the temperature to a high setting like 30°C to keep them open all the time. Use the remaining TRVs in rooms like bedrooms and kitchens for individual temperature control.

Balancing your radiators is often a process of trial and error, and you may need to slightly open or close lockshield valves to achieve a fully balanced system. Proceed with caution, as incorrect adjustments can worsen the imbalance, causing some areas to overheat and others to remain cold.

For optimal results, consider hiring a qualified professional. They have the expertise, experience, probes and specialised tools to accurately balance your radiator system, ensuring consistent and efficient heat distribution.

By grasping the importance of balanced radiators and ensuring proper maintenance and adjustments, you can optimise your heat pump system for comfort throughout your home. Remember, a balanced system enhances comfort and energy efficiency.

Understanding and identifying the index circuit in your heating system is essential for effective radiator balancing, whether you're a keen DIY-er or simply aiming to get the most out of your system.

Index Circuit

The index circuit is crucial for the proper functioning of your heating system. It's the circuit with the highest resistance to water flow, meaning it requires the most pump pressure to deliver heat effectively. This doesn't necessarily mean it's the longest circuit in your home, as factors like pipe size and radiator demand also play a role.

The index circuit is essentially the "hungriest" part of your heating system, requiring the highest flow rate to overcome resistance and adequately heat the connected space. By identifying and properly balancing the index circuit, you ensure that all other circuits receive the right amount of heat as well. Think of it as setting the standard for the rest of your heating system, ensuring efficient and even distribution of heat throughout your home.

Balancing a heating system, particularly working from the index circuit backwards, involves several critical steps, and this can be a complex process:

- Calculate the Required Flow Rate: For each radiator, calculate the flow rate needed to satisfy the heat output and Delta T (Δ) - usually 5°C for heat pumps. This initial step sets the groundwork for assessing the demands across the system.

- Assess Friction Loss in Each Feed: Each circuit or feed in the heating system will experience friction loss, which is dependent on factors like pipe length, diameter and flow rate. Calculating this loss is crucial to understand how much pressure is lost as water travels through the system.

- Work from the Extremities: Start at the furthest points of the system (the extremities) and add up the flow rates of each radiator to determine the cumulative flow rate in each primary branch. This approach helps in understanding the flow dynamics throughout the system.

- Calculate Friction Loss for Each Primary Branch: Taking into account the total length of the pipe installed in each section, calculate the friction loss for each primary branch. This calculation is vital for determining how much pressure the distribution pump needs to overcome these losses.
- Determine the Index Circuit: By adding the friction losses from each circuit, identify the index circuit - the one with the highest total friction loss. This circuit will dictate the minimum pump pressure required for adequate flow throughout the system.
- Incorporate Fittings Allowance: Add an additional 50% to account for friction loss due to fittings. This percentage is an assumption and may vary based on the specific installation and types of fittings used.

Working from the index circuit backwards when balancing heat emitters is essential for several reasons:
- Efficiency: It ensures that the most demanding circuit receives the necessary flow, which sets a baseline for the rest of the system.
- Uniform Heating: This method helps in achieving a more uniform heating experience throughout the property, as it ensures that all circuits are adequately fed based on the demand of the index circuit.
- Energy Savings: Proper balancing reduces unnecessary pump speed and pressure, leading to energy savings and reduced wear on the heating system.

Balancing a heating system, especially when working from the index circuit backward, involves precise steps, careful calculations and a solid understanding of the process. While dedicated DIY enthusiasts may find this achievable, it can be quite complex. If you're struggling to balance your system, it's always best to enlist the help of a professional heating engineer. Once your system is properly balanced, it should remain that way unless you make significant changes to your heating setup. This will save you time and frustration, ensuring optimal comfort and efficiency throughout your home.

Low Temperature System Design

Even if your heat pump is already installed - and you're reading this book for guidance - it's essential to assess whether it was set up correctly, especially if it replaced a fossil fuel boiler. This is particularly important if you suspect your system isn't running efficiently, struggling to heat your home adequately or costing more than anticipated.

Correct Radiator Sizing and Flow Rates

The foundation of a well-designed low-temperature heating system lies in the correct sizing of your radiators because they are essential for meeting your home's heating needs. Equally important are the flow rates, which determine how effectively heat is delivered throughout your living spaces. Undersized radiators or inadequate flow rates can result in a chilly home, an overworked heat pump and ultimately higher energy bills.

To ensure your radiators are up to the task, it's crucial to consider the heat loss of each room and select radiators with a sufficient surface area to compensate. Bigger isn't always better; it's about finding the right balance between size and heat output. Similarly, flow rates must be carefully calculated to ensure an adequate flow of hot water through each radiator, delivering consistent warmth to every corner of your home.

Unleashing the Power of Uncontrolled Flow

For optimal performance, your heating system should prioritise uncontrolled emitters, radiators and distribution circuits. This open-zone, free-flow approach ensures an even distribution of heat and minimises potential bottlenecks within your system.

Consider limiting control to specific areas like bedrooms, where individual temperature preferences may vary. In contrast, communal spaces like bathrooms, landings, halls and living areas benefit from uncontrolled flow, maintaining consistent warmth throughout. By striking this balance, you'll optimise your system's efficiency and create a comfortable environment in every corner of your home.

Thermostat Placement and Control Strategy

The thermostat, sensor or controller that governs your heat pump plays a crucial role in maintaining a comfortable home. For optimal performance, it should be strategically placed in a common area, ideally about 1.5 meters (5 feet) off the floor. This location allows it to accurately gauge the average temperature of your living spaces, ensuring the heat pump responds appropriately to your needs. By placing the control device in a central location, you avoid the risk of it being influenced by localised heat sources or drafts, leading to more efficient and comfortable heating throughout your home.

The control strategy for your heating system should be customised based on the building type and its thermal properties. Different properties benefit from different approaches, ensuring optimal efficiency and comfort. Here's a rough guide to give you a better idea.

For new builds with low thermal mass, such as those with lightweight construction and efficient insulation, load compensation is ideal:

- Radiator Systems: Load compensation adjusts the heat output based on the current heating demand, ensuring consistent indoor temperatures without overheating.
- Low Thermal Mass Overlay Underfloor Heating: Load compensation ensures the system heats quickly and efficiently, responding to temperature changes promptly.

New builds with medium thermal mass, which retain heat better due to heavier construction materials, benefit from a combination of strategies. Ideally, they should employ both weather and load compensation. Weather compensation adjusts the system based on external temperatures, while load compensation fine-tunes it according to internal demand, balancing comfort and efficiency.

Solid brick cavity builds (1930s to 1980s) typically have moderate thermal mass due to their brick construction and cavity walls:

- Radiator Systems: Use load compensation to adjust heat output to the current demand, preventing overheating and reducing energy waste.
- Low Thermal Mass Overlay Underfloor Heating: Load compensation ensures the system heats efficiently and maintains a comfortable indoor temperature.
- Medium Thermal Mass Underfloor Systems: Combine load and weather compensation to adjust to both internal demand and external temperature changes, optimising energy use and comfort.

Older buildings with solid walls and thick underfloor heating systems require a different approach:
- Weather Compensation: Adjusts the system based on external temperatures, ensuring the building remains warm without wasting energy.
- Modulating Control: Incorporate modulating control to adjust the heating output based on internal and external temperature variations, providing precise temperature regulation and enhancing comfort.

Commissioning the System

Correct commissioning is the final, crucial step to ensure your heating system's maximum flow rate can deliver the necessary energy under all design conditions. Unfortunately, we're increasingly seeing cases on the Renewable Heating Hub forums where systems haven't been properly commissioned before handover.

To verify that your system is operating correctly, particularly if you have metering equipment installed, you can check your flow rates. Here are some guidelines to help you assess your system's performance:
- Recommended Flow Rate: For example, a 5 kW demand should have a flow rate of 14 L/min with the pump on full and all control valves open.
- Minimum Flow Rate: Ensure even at minimum demand, the flow rates, such as 12 L/min for a 5 kW output, are sufficient to maintain efficiency and prevent system strain.

By adhering to flow rate guidelines, you can ensure your heating system is properly commissioned and operating at peak efficiency. Proper commissioning not only maximises your system's performance but also extends its lifespan and reduces the likelihood of issues down the line.

Is Your Heat Pump Undersized?

Are you constantly battling a persistent chill in your home, even when your heat pump seems to be running nonstop at full speed? Are your energy bills unexpectedly high? While it might not be what you want to hear, these could be telltale signs that your heat pump is simply not powerful enough to effectively heat your home.

Heat pumps are often selected by installers based on their maximum output under ideal conditions, as specified in their product literature. However, these conditions are seldom reflective of the typical operating environment, especially during the winter months.

Let's illustrate this: A heat pump boasting an 18 kW rating might only deliver around 12 kW when the air temperature outside dips to 7°C. As temperatures plummet further, so does the heat pump's output. At a bone-chilling -7°C, that same heat pump might only manage 10 kW.

This real-world drop in performance can have serious consequences. If your installer estimated your home needs 20 kW of heat at -3.3°C to stay warm, and your heat pump falls short of that during cold snaps, you're potentially dealing with an undersized system.

Consequences of an Undersized Heat Pump

- **Inadequate Heating:** The most obvious problem is that the heat pump fails to adequately heat your home, particularly during the coldest days when you need it most.
- **Increased Energy Costs:** An undersized unit needs to work harder and longer to meet the heating demand, which can significantly increase your energy consumption and costs.
- **Wear and Tear:** Continuous operation without adequate modulation puts extra stress on the heat pump, potentially leading to a shorter lifespan for the unit.

If you suspect your heat pump might be undersized:
- Review Performance Data: Start by consulting the installation manual or contacting the manufacturer to obtain detailed performance data for your specific heat pump model. This information is often found on a plate attached to the unit itself and might look something like this:

Output @ Air 7/2/-7/-10°C & Water 35°C: 8.58/ 10.92/ 12.13/ 10.85 kW
Input @ Air 7/2/-7/-10°C & water 35°C: 1.80 / 3.36 / 4.53 / 4.52 kW
COP @ Air 7/2/-7/-10°C & water 35°C: 4.76 / 3.25 / 2.68 / 2.40

These figures reveal how your heat pump's output (the heat it delivers) and efficiency (COP) change as the outside air temperature drops. If the output significantly decreases in colder weather, it may be undersized.

- Consult a Professional: If the signs point towards an undersized heat pump, don't hesitate to consult with a qualified installer (not the one that installed your system). A competent installer can thoroughly assess your home's unique heating requirements and the capacity of your current system. Through calculations, they can determine if your heat pump's size aligns with the specific demands of your property, considering factors such as insulation quality, local climate conditions and your desired comfort levels.

If your original installer is reluctant or unable to help, don't lose hope. Seek an independent review from another qualified professional. This unbiased assessment is crucial to uncover any underlying issues with your heating system and provide you with a clear understanding of the situation.

Should your heat pump be relatively new and you're facing resistance or a lack of support from the installer or manufacturer, remember that you have options. Escalating your concerns through consumer protection agencies, the Microgeneration Certification Scheme (MCS) or other relevant regulatory bodies can help you find a resolution and ensure your investment delivers the warmth and comfort you expect.

- Consider a Supplemental Solution: If replacing your undersized heat pump isn't immediately feasible, explore other avenues to improve your home's comfort and energy efficiency. Supplemental heating solutions, such as infrared space heaters, can provide a temporary boost of warmth during particularly cold days.

  However, addressing the root cause of heat loss is key to a long-term solution. Investing in improved insulation for your walls, roof and floors can significantly reduce heat loss, making it easier for your existing heat pump to maintain a comfortable temperature and potentially lower your energy bills. This proactive approach not only enhances comfort but also extends the lifespan of your heat pump by easing its workload.

Understanding the sizing and efficiency of your heat pump under realistic conditions is crucial for maintaining a comfortable and cost-effective home environment. If your house is not warming up adequately, take the time to evaluate whether your heat pump truly fits your needs, even though it's a challenging realisation, especially after a costly installation. Don't be afraid to question your installer about this. If you're still battling, visit the Renewable Heating Hub forums - https://renewableheatinghub.co.uk - where other experienced homeowners will be able to help you and offer practical advice.

Make Your Own Notes Here:

Is Your Heat Pump Oversized?

It's a less frequent, yet equally problematic, concern that homeowners might have an oversized heat pump for their home. While much of the focus is on the risks of undersizing, oversized systems bring their own set of challenges.

Understanding Oversizing

Similar to an undersized heat pump, an oversized one can also be inefficient, albeit in a different way. Heat pumps thrive when they operate continuously at a steady pace, gently warming your home over time. However, an oversized heat pump may heat your home too quickly, causing it to shut off prematurely. This frequent on-and-off cycling, known as "short cycling," is detrimental to efficiency.

Consider this: an 18 kW heat pump might seem like a wise choice to guarantee warmth during the coldest days, especially for a smaller home. But if your home needs significantly less heat during milder temperatures, the heat pump will be operating outside its ideal efficiency range. It will heat your home rapidly, then shut off before completing a full heating cycle, only to turn on again as soon as the temperature drops. This constant starting and stopping is like a car repeatedly accelerating and braking - it wastes energy and puts unnecessary strain on the engine (or in this case, the heat pump).

The Consequences

Operating an oversized heat pump can lead to various problems:
- Short Cycling: When a heat pump is too large, it heats the space too quickly and shuts off, only to turn on again shortly after.
- Higher Initial Costs: Bigger units are more expensive to purchase and install. If the capacity exceeds what is necessary, you're incurring unnecessary upfront costs.

- Inefficiency and Higher Running Costs: Oversized units can be less efficient due to short cycling and may lead to increased energy costs over time, negating the benefits of choosing a heat pump in the first place.

What You Can Do
If you're concerned that your heat pump may be oversized:
- Monitor Cycling Patterns: Pay attention to how often your heat pump cycles on and off. If it seems too frequent, it could be an indication that the unit is too large.
- Consult a Professional: A competent heating engineer or professional installer can assess whether your heat pump's size is appropriate for your home and recommend solutions. This may require calling someone else other than your installer to verify if this is the case.
- Adjustment and Zoning: In some cases, adjustments can be made to your system's settings to better regulate its output. Zoning, which involves dividing your home into different heating zones, can also be a viable solution to utilise excess capacity more effectively. Your heating professional can advise on the best course of action for your specific situation.

Properly sizing your heat pump is a critical step in achieving a comfortable, efficient and long-lasting heating system for your home. An oversized heat pump, much like its undersized counterpart, can wreak havoc on your comfort and wallet. It's not simply about ensuring your home stays warm; it's about achieving that warmth efficiently and ensuring your system operates smoothly for years to come.

If you notice your heat pump cycling on and off frequently, don't dismiss it as a minor quirk. It could be a sign of oversizing, and addressing it promptly is key to avoiding the potential pitfalls. By understanding the consequences of oversizing and taking the necessary steps to assess and rectify the situation, you'll not only optimise your energy usage but also ensure your heat pump investment pays off in the long run.

Antifreeze Valves vs. Glycol

In the UK, it's customary for many installers to use glycol (antifreeze) solutions in central heating systems. This practice is sometimes driven by manufacturer recommendations, especially for colder regions, where freezing temperatures pose a higher risk. While glycol provides a layer of freeze protection, it's crucial to weigh its pros and cons against an alternative solution: antifreeze valves.

The Glycol Tradeoff

Glycol undoubtedly offers protection against freezing, but it's important to understand that this safeguard comes with a few compromises:

- Reduced Efficiency: Glycol, being thicker than water, creates more resistance within your pipes. This means your pump has to work harder to circulate the fluid, resulting in a 20-30% increase in pump power consumption. This directly translates to higher energy bills and a less eco-friendly operation.
- Maintenance Demands: Introducing glycol to your system isn't a "set it and forget it" solution. The concentration needs to be monitored and maintained to ensure optimal performance and prevent corrosion. This can entail regular testing, top-ups and potential headaches down the line.
- Environmental Concerns: Glycol, particularly ethylene glycol, can be harmful to the environment if spilled. It requires careful handling and disposal to avoid contamination of soil and water sources.

Propylene Glycol vs. Ethylene Glycol

When it comes to glycol, there are two primary options for heating systems: propylene glycol and ethylene glycol. Propylene glycol boasts the advantage of being less toxic, making it a safer choice for accidental spills or leaks. However, this safety comes at a cost - propylene glycol has a higher viscosity than ethylene glycol. This increased thickness means it requires even more pumping power to circulate effectively, further impacting your energy consumption.

Antifreeze Valves: A Potential Alternative

Antifreeze valves present a compelling alternative to glycol for safeguarding your heat pump system against freezing temperatures. These devices automatically drain the water from your system when the temperature dips below a predetermined threshold, effectively preventing the formation of ice and the subsequent damage it can cause.

Unlike glycol, antifreeze valves don't compromise your system's efficiency by altering the viscosity of the fluid. They also eliminate the ongoing maintenance headaches associated with glycol concentration checks and top-ups.

However, it's crucial to acknowledge a potential vulnerability. If a power outage occurs during freezing temperatures while the system is drained, there's a risk of pipe damage. This scenario highlights the importance of having a reliable power source or backup plan for your heat pump system in case of prolonged outages.

Despite this caveat, antifreeze valves offer a compelling solution for those seeking a more efficient and maintenance-free approach to freeze protection. They eliminate the drawbacks of glycol while providing peace of mind in most scenarios.

The decision between glycol and antifreeze valves for your heat pump system isn't a one-size-fits-all answer. It depends on various factors, including your specific climate, the type of heat pump you have and the manufacturer's recommendations.

To ensure you make the best choice for your home and system, it's crucial to consult with a competent installer. They can assess your individual needs and provide expert guidance on whether glycol or antifreeze valves are the most suitable freeze protection solution for you. Remember, an informed decision is a wise decision, and seeking professional advice can help you avoid costly mistakes and ensure your heat pump system operates efficiently and reliably for years to come.

Insulation, Comfort & Efficiency

Proper insulation is a critical factor in ensuring the optimal performance and comfort of your air source heat pump. Insulation acts as a thermal barrier, preventing heat from escaping through walls, roofs floors and windows.

By investing in adequate insulation, you can significantly reduce heat loss, allowing your heat pump to operate more efficiently. This means it won't have to work as hard to maintain your desired temperature, resulting in lower energy consumption and reduced heating bills. Additionally, well-insulated homes experience more consistent temperatures, eliminating cold spots and drafts, and ensuring a comfortable living environment throughout the year.

DIY Insulation Tips

Here are some simple, do-it-yourself projects to improve your home's insulation:

- Seal the Leaks: Like a leaky bucket, a draughty home wastes energy. Take a walk around your home on a windy day and feel for drafts around windows, doors, electrical outlets and plumbing fixtures. If you have access to a thermal imaging camera, use it to identify areas where heat is escaping or cold air is entering. These cameras can highlight temperature differences, making it easier to spot and address leaks. Seal these leaks using caulk, filler, weatherstripping or draft excluders. Don't forget the gap under your front door.
- Weatherstrip Your Windows: Older windows might lack proper weatherstripping, allowing precious warm air to escape. Replacing worn-out weatherstripping with a modern version can make a significant difference.
- Insulate Your Loft: The loft is a major culprit for heat loss. Consider adding loft insulation or topping up existing insulation to

the recommended depth for your region. Check with local building regulations for specific requirements. While some loft insulation projects are DIY-friendly, thicker installations might require professional assistance.
- Insulate Your Hot Water Tank: A well-insulated hot water tank retains heat more effectively, reducing energy consumption and workload on your heat pump. Most hot water tanks for heat pumps come pre-insulated, but you can often add an additional insulating jacket for further efficiency gains.
- Clever Use of Curtains: Thick curtains can act as an additional layer of insulation during winter especially on leaky windows in period properties. Draw them closed at night to trap heat inside.
- Address Cavities and Wall Voids: If your home has any exposed cavities or wall voids, consider filling them with insulating materials like cellulose fibre or rockwool insulation. These hidden pockets of air can be sources of heat loss.
- Upgrade Your Doors: For older or draughty exterior doors, replacing them with well-insulated and weather-sealed doors can significantly improve overall home insulation and reduce the workload on your heating system.
- Maximise Natural Light and Heat Gains: During winter days, open curtains and blinds on south-facing windows to allow natural sunlight and heat to warm your home passively. This reduces reliance on your ASHP during sunnier periods.
- Cover Draughty Floorboards: If you have gaps in your floorboards, consider filling them with a suitable sealant or covering them with rugs or carpets. This will help prevent drafts and heat loss from below.
- Use Rugs and Carpets: In addition to covering floorboards, adding rugs and carpets to uninsulated floors provides an extra layer of insulation, making your floors feel warmer and reducing heat loss.
- Mind the Gap: Seal gaps around pipes and cables where they enter your home's exterior walls. These seemingly small openings can be sources of heat loss.
- Plug Unused Chimneys: If you have a fireplace you rarely or never use, consider installing a chimney balloon or similar device to block

the chimney when not in use. This prevents warm air from escaping up the flue.
- Bleed Your Radiators: Air trapped within radiators can create cold spots and hinder heat distribution. Regularly bleeding your radiators (releasing trapped air) ensures optimal heat flow and efficient heat pump operation.

Insulation + ASHP = Improved Performance

By making these simple improvements and ensuring your home is properly insulated, you create a powerful partnership between your heat pump and your home. This synergy allows your heat pump to operate more efficiently, maintaining a comfortable temperature with minimal energy use. The result is a warmer, cosier home with lower energy bills and a reduced environmental footprint.

Make Your Own Notes Here:

Regular Maintenance Schedule

Heat pumps require regular maintenance to function efficiently and last for their expected lifespan. Like any mechanical system, the more a heat pump is switched on and off or pushed to its maximum, the shorter its lifespan becomes. The extra load on the compressor also puts additional strain on the electronics.

Regular upkeep can prevent minor issues from escalating into major problems, saving you from costly repairs and ensuring consistent comfort in your home. For instance, if the evaporator is dirty, it cannot collect heat effectively, resulting in extra load on the compressor and electrical components. Lack of maintenance might decrease the lifespan of a heat pump.

When it comes to replacing the system, most parts should be accessible and replaceable. However, there may come a point where spending hundreds or even thousands annually on repairs becomes less economical than replacing the entire system. Many manufacturers now offer extended warranties of 7 to 10 years, contingent on proper annual maintenance. This suggests that with correct upkeep, a heat pump should last at least 10 years, and ideally 15-20 years.

A well-maintained heat pump not only performs better but also operates more efficiently, which can translate to lower energy bills. Regular maintenance can identify potential problems early on, preventing unexpected breakdowns and maximising the lifespan of your investment. By following a regular maintenance schedule, you'll be taking a proactive approach to ensure your heat pump continues to deliver reliable, efficient, and comfortable heating for years to come.

Your Heat Pump's Annual Check-Up

The cornerstone of maintaining your heat pump's health and performance is an annual professional service. Schedule a thorough inspection by a qualified heat pump engineer at least once a year, ideally before the heating season begins. This proactive approach ensures your system is ready to tackle the demands of winter and identifies potential issues before they escalate into costly repairs.

Here's what a professional service typically encompasses:

- Internal Component Inspection: The engineer should examine the heat pump's inner workings, including the compressor, evaporator coil and condenser coil. They'll look for signs of wear, potential leaks or any other anomalies that could impact performance.
- Cleaning and Adjustments: Crucial components like the evaporator and condenser coils should be cleaned to remove dust, dirt and debris that can hinder efficient heat transfer. The engineer should also fine-tune the system's settings to optimise operation if required.

Seasonal DIY Maintenance

Beyond the annual professional check-up, there are several seasonal tasks you can perform to ensure your heat pump operates at its best year-round:

- Spring Cleaning: As winter's chill fades and temperatures rise, take a moment to inspect your ASHP's outdoor unit. Clear away any accumulated leaves, debris or vegetation that may have gathered during the colder months. Ensure there's adequate clearance around the unit (at least 600mm is recommended, but consult your manual for specific requirements) to allow for unrestricted airflow.
- Autumn Preparation: Before winter's icy grip returns, give your outdoor unit another thorough once-over. Remove any leaves, debris or cobwebs that might have accumulated over summer. If you live in an area prone to snowfall, be vigilant about keeping the unit free of snow and ice buildup. This prevents operational issues and ensures your heat pump is ready to tackle the coldest days.

The Rewards of Regular Maintenance

By committing to this maintenance schedule, you're not just ticking boxes off a to-do list. You're investing in the long-term health and efficiency of your heat pump. Here's what you can expect in return:

- Enhanced Efficiency: Regular cleaning and servicing ensure your heat pump runs at peak performance, extracting maximum heat from the air with minimal energy consumption. This translates to significant savings on your energy bills and a reduced carbon footprint.

- Extended Lifespan: Just like regular checkups can prolong a human life, proactive maintenance keeps your heat pump in tip-top shape. By preventing premature wear and tear, you're potentially adding years to your system's lifespan, delaying the need for costly replacements or repairs.
- Peace of Mind: Knowing that your ASHP is well-maintained offers peace of mind, especially during the coldest months. You can rest assured that your home will be warm and comfortable, no matter how low the temperature drops.
- Reduced Repair Costs: Small issues, if left unchecked, can escalate into major problems. Regular maintenance helps catch these issues early, allowing for timely and less expensive repairs. This proactive approach saves you money in the long run and prevents unexpected breakdowns that could disrupt your daily life.

Make Your Own Notes Here:

Home & Emergency Insurance

Your air source heat pump represents a significant investment in your home's comfort and energy efficiency. Just as you wouldn't leave your car or other valuable possessions unprotected, it's essential to ensure your heat pump is adequately covered against unforeseen events. This is where home insurance steps in, offering financial protection in case of damage, theft, vandalism or unexpected malfunctions.

Check Your Policy: Don't Assume Coverage

It's easy to assume that your heat pump falls under your general home insurance policy, but that's not always the case. While most policies readily cover traditional gas and oil boilers for damage or emergency repairs, we've seen a concerning trend in the UK: some policies explicitly exclude heat pumps, while others have ambiguous clauses. This means that if your heat pump is damaged due to a storm, vandalism, or even a simple malfunction, you might be left footing a hefty repair bill because they won't cover it.

Emergency Cover

In addition to damage or theft coverage, it's equally important to ensure your insurer covers your heat pump under their emergency cover. This type of coverage typically provides assistance with repairs if your primary heating source fails, leaving you without heat or hot water. Without this protection, you could face significant inconvenience and expense if your system breaks down in the middle of winter. Imagine being left without heating during the coldest months - it's not just uncomfortable but can also lead to other issues, such as frozen pipes. Make sure to review your insurance policy thoroughly and speak to your insurer to confirm that your heat pump is adequately covered for all potential scenarios. This proactive step can save you a lot of trouble and expense in the long run.

Shop Around and Double-Check with Your Insurer

Given the escalating cost of heat pumps, it's essential to be proactive about insurance coverage. Don't just assume you're covered; take the time to review your policy carefully. Look for specific mentions of heat pumps in both the general coverage and emergency cover sections. Many policies speak about primary heating sources, but many don't recognise heat pumps as falling into that category. If you're unsure, reach out to your insurance provider and ask them directly. Better still - get it in writing.

If you find that your current policy doesn't cover your heat pump, don't despair. There are insurers in the UK that offer comprehensive coverage for heat pumps, including both damage/theft and emergency repairs. Shopping around and comparing policies can help you find the right fit for your needs and budget.

Key Questions to Ask Your Insurer:

- Is my heat pump covered for damage or theft under my existing policy?
- Does my emergency cover include heat pump breakdowns and repairs?
- Are there specific exclusions or limitations related to heat pump coverage?
- What is the process for filing a claim if my heat pump is damaged or malfunctions?

Troubleshooting & Error Codes

Even the most reliable ASHP can occasionally hiccup. Straightforward troubleshooting for common heat pump issues can help you resolve them without immediately turning to professional assistance. Learn to identify and fix typical problems, including error codes on the display panel, unusual noises or reduced heating effectiveness. This involves diagnosing the problem, carrying out simple solutions such as resetting the system, clearing blockages, adjusting settings and recognising when the expertise of a qualified technician is needed for more complex issues.

Remember: Safety First!

Before attempting any troubleshooting steps, <u>always</u> ensure the heat pump is turned off and disconnected from the power source. Never attempt electrical work or disassemble components unless you possess the necessary qualifications. If you're unsure about any step, consult a qualified professional. Your safety is paramount.

Consulting Your User Manual

Your first line of defence is your user manual. It should contain a dedicated section explaining the specific error codes associated with your heat pump model. While understanding common error code categories can provide a basic understanding of potential problems, avoid the temptation to self-diagnose and attempt complex repairs.

A qualified heat pump engineer possesses the expertise and tools to accurately diagnose the root cause of the error code, ensuring a swift and hopefully effective repair.

Understanding Error Codes

Your air source heat pump uses a display panel to communicate its status at all times. If something goes awry, this panel should show error codes or alarms that can help you pinpoint the issue. Think of them as your heat pump's way of saying something's not quite right.

We will walk you through some of the most common error codes and offer basic troubleshooting tips. But remember, each heat pump model is unique and error codes can vary.

Common Error Codes and Solutions
- Communication Error: This error indicates an issue with the connection between the indoor and outdoor units. Inspect the wiring for any signs of damage or loose connections. Secure any loose wires and ensure all connections are tight.
- Temperature Sensor Fault: A faulty temperature sensor can disrupt your ASHP's ability to maintain desired temperatures. Check the sensors for signs of physical damage or disconnection. Sometimes, a simple system reset can resolve the issue. Consult your user manual for instructions on restarting your heat pump.
- Compressor Overload: The compressor is the heart of your air source heat pump, and if it becomes overloaded, the unit will shut down to prevent damage. If this happens, turn off the ASHP and allow the compressor to cool down for at least 30 minutes before restarting. While the unit is off, check for any obstructions blocking airflow around the indoor and outdoor units. Ensure vents are clear and that the fan is working. If the problem persists and the compressor overloads again, turn off the heat pump and contact a qualified heating engineer. A professional assessment is essential to diagnose and resolve any underlying problems, such as refrigerant issues, electrical faults or mechanical failures.
- Low Pressure Fault: A low pressure fault indicates insufficient refrigerant in the system. Refrigerant leaks or blockages in the pipes or filters can cause this issue. Do _not_ attempt to fix refrigerant leaks yourself. These require a qualified service technician with specialised tools and training to diagnose and repair. Contact a technician to address a low pressure fault.

- Low Flow Rate: This error code indicates a problem with water circulation within the system, which is crucial for efficient heat pump operation. Look for blockages in the pumps or filters, airlocks within the pipe or ensure all valves in the system are fully open. It's important to note that air source heat pumps require a minimum water flow rate (as discussed earlier) to function properly to avoid compressor damage. If you've addressed potential blockages and airlocks but the error persists, there's a possibility that the flow rate sensor itself might be malfunctioning. This sensor monitors water circulation and sends a signal to the controller. A faulty sensor might provide inaccurate readings, triggering the error code even when the flow rate is adequate. In such cases, or if the troubleshooting steps don't resolve the issue, it's best to contact a qualified service technician for further diagnosis and repair.
- Electrical Fault: Sometimes, a power surge or loose electrical connection can trigger an electrical fault. Try power cycling the system by turning it off completely and then waiting a few minutes before restarting. If the error persists after a power cycle, ensure all electrical connections are secure. If you're uncomfortable checking electrical connections, it's best to contact a qualified electrician.
- Defrost Mode Error: During cold weather operation, your heat pump may enter defrost mode periodically to prevent ice buildup on the outdoor unit. However, if the defrost cycle seems to be occurring excessively, it could indicate restricted airflow around the outdoor unit. Ensure there are no obstructions blocking airflow and that the recommended clearances around the unit are maintained according to the manufacturer's specifications.

This list addresses common error codes that homeowners might encounter from time to time. If you have an error code not covered here, or if the troubleshooting steps don't resolve the issue, consult your user manual for further guidance. For complex repairs or situations involving refrigerant leaks, it's always best to contact a qualified service technician to diagnose and fix the problem. Most manufacturers have call centres and help lines you can call and they may be able to advise you how to deal with an error.

Errors are common and we've addressed many of them on the Renewable Heating Hub Forums where we also have solutions to get you back up and running: https://renewableheatinghub.co.uk/forums

Know Your Limits

While these troubleshooting tips can help you tackle minor issues, it's important to recognise your limits. If you're uncertain about any step or the problem persists, don't hesitate to contact a qualified heat pump engineer. Prompt action can prevent a minor issue from turning into a major (and expensive) repair. Additionally, attempting DIY repairs beyond basic troubleshooting may void your warranty. Here's when to seek professional help:

- Unfamiliar Error Codes: If the error code displayed on your control panel isn't listed in your user manual (this does happen) or you're unsure of its meaning, consult a qualified heat pump engineer.
- Complex Troubleshooting Steps: If the user manual recommends troubleshooting steps that seem complex or involve electrical work, it's best to leave it to a professional because any damage you cause might void the unit's warranty.
- Persistent Errors: If the error code persists even after trying the recommended troubleshooting steps, professional intervention is necessary to diagnose and fix the underlying issue.

Peace & Quiet

While air source heat pumps are known for their energy efficiency, they're not always silent operators. Understanding the sources of noise and implementing strategies to minimise it is crucial for creating a peaceful and comfortable living environment.

Understanding ASHP Noise

There are two main sources of noise generation in an air source heat pump:

- The Compressor: This is the heart of the system, responsible for compressing refrigerant. While modern compressors are quieter than ever, they can still produce a humming sound. The casings on most ASHP models are also usually insulted to limit noise.
- The Fan: The outdoor unit fan circulates air across the condenser coil to release heat. Fan noise can vary depending on the unit's operating speed and the outdoor temperature.

Minimising Noise Levels

Here are some strategies to keep your air source heat pump operating quietly:

- Strategic Placement: During installation, ensure the outdoor unit is positioned away from your bedroom windows or any other living areas where noise might be disruptive. Equally so, make sure they aren't pointed ay neighbouring properties where they can be a nuisance. Maintaining a minimum clearance of 600mm (this may vary from heat pump to heat pump) around the unit allows for optimal airflow and can help reduce noise levels.
- Anti-vibration Mounts: A common complaint among heat pump owners is the transmission of vibrations through the structure of their homes, especially when the unit is installed on a wooden deck or close to the house. Anti-vibration mounts or pads offer a simple

and effective solution to this problem. By absorbing the vibrations generated by the heat pump, these mounts significantly reduce the noise that travels into your home or disturbs your neighbours. Unfortunately, anti-vibration mounts don't usually come standard with some heat pump models and often need to be ordered separately. So, if you're experiencing excessive noise from your heat pump, check if anti-vibration mounts have been installed. If not, consider adding them to significantly reduce the noise and vibrations.

- Regular Maintenance: Schedule regular maintenance by a qualified heat pump engineer. Regular cleaning of the outdoor unit's coils and fins ensures efficient operation, which can minimise noise generation. Worn bearings or loose components can also contribute to noise, and a professional service can identify and address these issues.
- Landscaping Solutions: Planting shrubs or trees strategically around the outdoor unit (but not too close to obstruct airflow) can create a natural sound barrier. Choose evergreen varieties that will provide year-round noise reduction.
- Drying logs: We've observed some innovative homeowners utilising their air source heat pump to aid in drying logs. By building a log store just a meter or two away from the ASHP fan, the air expelled by the fan helps dry the logs. Additionally, the log store can act as a sound barrier, helping to muffle the noise from the ASHP. If you like the idea and decide to do this, ensure that the log store doesn't obstruct airflow or impede the ASHP's performance.

When to Call a Professional

Even the most reliable and well-maintained air source heat pumps can experience issues. It's crucial to recognise when DIY solutions won't suffice and seeking professional assistance is the wisest course of action.

Signs of Trouble

While troubleshooting minor heat pump issues can be a rewarding DIY experience, certain warning signs indicate that it's time to call in the experts:

- Abnormal Noises: Your ASHP should operate with a quiet hum. If you hear unusual noises like grinding, clanging or loud vibrations, shut down the system immediately and call a professional. These noises could indicate loose components or internal damage, all requiring expert attention.
- Reduced Heating Performance: Is your home not getting as warm as usual? If there are no errors on your control panel or any other obvious problems, a qualified engineer should be able diagnose the cause and restore your comfort.
- Leaking Fluids: Any leaks from your heat pump or associated pipework are a cause for concern. Shut down the system immediately and contact a professional. Leaks can indicate damaged pipes, loose connections or even a malfunctioning compressor, all requiring professional repair.
- System Shutdown and Error Codes: Most modern ASHPs often display error codes when they encounter a malfunction. While your user manual might offer a basic explanation of the error code, deciphering the root cause and fixing complex issues is often best left to a trained engineer.
- Burning Smells: Any burning smells emanating from your heat pump are a serious concern and indicate a potential electrical issue

or overheating. Shut down the system immediately and call a professional right away to avoid further damage.
- Ice or Frost Buildup: Keep a watchful eye on the outdoor unit, especially during colder months. A thin layer of frost is normal, but excessive ice buildup could signal a problem, such as a malfunctioning defrost cycle or a refrigerant leak. If you notice significant ice accumulation that's not completely melting away, contact a qualified heat pump engineer to investigate and resolve the issue promptly.
- Tripped Fuse: If your heat pump repeatedly trips the fuse or RCD (the safety switch in your fuse box), it's a clear sign of an electrical problem. Don't attempt to fix this yourself; call a qualified electrician immediately to investigate.

The Benefits of Professional Intervention
Calling a qualified heat pump engineer offers several advantages:
- Accurate Diagnosis: Most heating professionals possess the expertise and tools to diagnose problems accurately, saving you time and money on unnecessary repairs.
- Proper Repairs: They have the training and experience to conduct repairs and replace damaged parts safely and effectively, ensuring your ASHP operates at peak performance.
- Warranty Considerations: Attempting DIY repairs on your ASHP might void the manufacturer's warranty. Consulting a qualified professional (preferably one that has been certified by your heat pump manufacturer) ensures any repairs maintain your warranty coverage.
- Safety: Heat pumps involve electrical and refrigerant systems, which can be dangerous if mishandled. A professional should have the knowledge and training to work safely with these components.
- Future Prevention: A professional service often includes recommendations for improving system efficiency and preventing future problems.

Manufacturer Support

If you're reading this book, chances are you already have a heat pump humming away in your home, courtesy of a chosen installer. However, not all installers offer the same level of post-installation support, and unfortunately, the same can be said for heat pump manufacturers. Some prioritise customer service, going above and beyond to troubleshoot issues and send out their own engineers, while others... well, they leave something to be desired.

Our forums at Renewable Heating Hub - https://renewableheatinghub.co.uk/forums - are filled with stories from homeowners who have been left in the lurch by installers (and manufacturers), especially when projects haven't gone smoothly. It's a frustrating situation, but it's becoming more common in the UK. So, what's a homeowner to do?

When Your Installer Goes AWOL, Call the Manufacturer

If you encounter any issues with your heat pump, your first instinct might be to panic. But remember, you're not alone in this. Your heat pump's manufacturer should be your first port of call and can often be a valuable resource, even if your installer isn't readily available or helpful. Whether you have simple questions about your system, need guidance on maintenance or are facing a major malfunction, don't hesitate to reach out to the manufacturer's customer support. Here's why manufacturer support can be a lifeline:

- Technical Expertise: Manufacturers know their products inside and out. They can often diagnose issues remotely or guide you through troubleshooting steps if the issue is relatively straightforward to fix.
- Warranty Coverage: Many manufacturers offer warranties that cover repairs or replacements for a certain period. Contacting them ensures you're taking advantage of this protection.

- Engineer Dispatch: In some cases, manufacturers will send out their own engineers to assess and fix problems, especially if the issue is complex or falls under warranty. While this level of support can vary from manufacturer to manufacturer, it's well within your rights to politely request this level of assistance. After all, it's their product that you've invested in, and they have a vested interest in ensuring its proper operation. Don't hesitate to advocate for yourself and ask for on-site assistance if you believe it's necessary - especially if your installer has abandoned you.
- Installer Pressure: A call from the manufacturer can sometimes pressure an unresponsive installer to fulfil their obligations, particularly if the installer is accredited by the manufacturer. Installers risk losing their accreditation or future business opportunities if they fail to meet the manufacturer's standards. This approach can be an effective way to ensure your concerns are addressed promptly and professionally.

How to Access Manufacturer Support

Most heat pump manufacturers offer dedicated customer support lines or online portals for technical assistance. These resources are designed to help you troubleshoot issues, answer questions about your system and access expert product advice. You can usually find contact information in your heat pump's user manual or on the manufacturer's website. Remember, manufacturer support is a valuable resource available to you, so don't hesitate to utilise it whenever you have questions or concerns about your heat pump.

Be Prepared: Gather Your Information

To make the most of your interaction with manufacturer support, have the following information ready:
- Model and Serial Number: This helps identify your specific heat pump and its warranty status.
- Installation Date: This can be important for warranty claims.
- Maintenance Records: Any records of previous service or repairs can provide context for your current issue.
- Error Codes: If your heat pump is displaying any error codes, note them down.

Manufacturers That Have Stepped Up

In an effort to equip you with the best information in this book, we reached out to all major heat pump manufacturers in the UK. The following brands responded to our request and have provided details on their customer service availability. Regrettably, we have observed on the Renewable Heating Hub forums that some brands are more supportive to homeowners than others. We hope that more brands will follow suit and strive to support homeowners more effectively, especially when issues arise with their systems and the support from their installers falls short.

- **Clivet**: In today's market, ensuring reliable support services for your home installations is paramount. Unfortunately, it is becoming increasingly common for homeowners to face challenges when installers do not provide the expected level of support. To address this, Clivet is committed to offering a robust network of Clivet-approved installers who can offer support services directly to homeowners. If you need help or support, please contact them directly by phone or email. They will then connect you with a Clivet-approved installer who will be more than happy to assist you. You can call them on 02392 381235 or email l.cleary@clivet.com

- **Mitsubishi**: As a leading manufacturer, Mitsubishi Electric's commitment extends beyond product excellence to comprehensive customer care. Should homeowners encounter challenges with after-install support, they offer dedicated home portal and home support channels, ensuring personalised resolution and a seamless experience. Through the Home Portal - https://ecodan.me.uk/homeownerportal - Mitsubishi provides numerous resources for confidence in home heating systems, additionally offering market-leading service plans to ensure Ecodan heat pump systems' upkeep and maximise efficiency. Prioritising customer satisfaction, they aim to inspire positive reviews on platforms like Trustpilot, influencing broader adoption. Positive experiences foster consumer confidence and dispel myths, making their technology more appealing to potential buyers.

- **NIBE**: NIBE heat pump owners can keep their heat pumps running optimally and spread the cost of servicing with NIBE's FlexiServ support package. Annual servicing ensures your heat pump operates smoothly and efficiently while preventing costly repairs and downtime. Available for new and existing NIBE heat pumps, whether in or out of warranty, FlexiServ provides peace of mind that your heat pump is taken care of. NIBE will keep track of when your next service is due and book a visit from one of its expertly trained engineers at a convenient time.
Visit https://www.nibe.co.uk to find out more.

While we all hope for smooth sailing with our heat pump installations, it's wise to be prepared for bumps in the road, even if it's a few years after the heat pump has been installed. By knowing how to access manufacturer support, you're empowering yourself to take control of your heating system and ensure it delivers the comfort and efficiency you deserve.

However, if you're facing an uphill battle with an unresponsive or unhelpful manufacturer, don't give up. Visit the Renewable Heating Hub forums and post your issues there. We'll raise these concerns directly with manufacturers (often publicly to exert additional pressure on them), using our platform to advocate for homeowners.

We understand that manufacturers cannot be held liable for every shoddy installation, but in most instances, installers are accredited or trained by the manufacturer themselves. This creates a shared responsibility to ensure that homeowners get their expensive heat pumps working properly and efficiently. Manufacturers have an ethical obligation to support their customers, especially when their accredited installers fall short.

Remember, your voice matters. By sharing your experiences and seeking help, you're not only improving your own situation but also contributing to a stronger, more accountable heat pump industry for everyone.

Heat Pumps, PV & Battery Storage

The integration of air source heat pumps with solar photovoltaic (PV) panels and battery storage presents a compelling opportunity for homeowners to create a highly efficient, sustainable and potentially cost-effective home energy system. This synergy leverages renewable solar energy to power your ASHP, significantly reducing reliance on the grid and minimising your carbon footprint.

During daylight hours, solar PV panels generate electricity from sunlight, which can be used to directly power your ASHP. This significantly reduces your reliance on grid electricity, which is often generated from fossil fuels, resulting in lower greenhouse gas emissions. However, solar energy generation is intermittent, and your heat pump may still require electricity during periods of low sunlight or at night. This is where battery storage plays a crucial role.

Battery storage systems enable you to store excess energy generated by your solar panels during peak production hours. This stored energy can then be utilised to power your heat pump during periods of low solar generation, ensuring a continuous and reliable supply of heat. By intelligently managing the flow of energy between your solar panels, battery storage and ASHP, you can optimise your system's performance and maximise your energy savings.

The Sustainable Trifecta

Integrating PV panels and battery storage with your air source heat pump establishes a cohesive and efficient energy ecosystem within your home. This interconnected system maximises the utilisation of renewable energy, reduces reliance on the grid and contributes to a more sustainable lifestyle. The process unfolds in a seamless cycle. During daylight hours, your solar PV panels harness the sun's energy, converting it into electricity. This clean, renewable electricity is then directly utilised to power your ASHP, reducing your dependence on grid-supplied electricity. Excess electricity generated by your solar panels, which exceeds your immediate needs, is stored in your battery system. When solar energy generation is low or nonexistent, such as during nighttime hours or cloudy days, the stored energy in your battery powers your ASHP.

Sustainable Upgrade Path
While the potential benefits of integrating heat pumps with solar PV and battery storage are undeniable, it is a costly investment and careful planning is essential to ensure a successful and efficient system:
- Assess Your Needs: Begin by thoroughly evaluating your home's energy consumption patterns. Analyse your electricity bills and consider your household's daily energy demands. Additionally, assess the suitability of your roof space for solar panels. Factors like size, orientation and shading can significantly impact solar energy generation. Consulting with a qualified professional can help you determine if this integrated approach is a viable option for your specific circumstances.
- System Design and Installation: Choosing a reputable installer with expertise in ASHPs, solar PV systems and battery storage is paramount. While a single installer might not be able to handle all aspects of the installation, ensure that the chosen professionals have the necessary experience and qualifications to seamlessly integrate these technologies for optimal performance.
- Financial Considerations: It's important to be aware that the initial investment for solar panels and battery storage can be substantial. However, it's equally important to consider the long-term savings on energy bills, potential government grants and the environmental benefits that come with a reduced carbon footprint.
- Limitations: While solar panels and battery storage can significantly offset your energy consumption, it's important to acknowledge that they probably won't fully power your ASHP overnight, especially during periods of low solar generation. However, even with this limitation, the integration of these technologies still plays a crucial role in reducing your reliance on the grid and enhancing the overall sustainability of your home energy system.

Electricity Tariffs

You already know that air source heat pumps are a fantastic way to heat your home efficiently. But did you know you can significantly reduce running costs and contribute to a more sustainable home energy setup by experimenting with time of use electricity tariffs?

Time-of-Use Tariffs

The UK energy market offers various electricity tariffs. Understanding them is key to finding the perfect fit for your heat pump and energy habits. Unlike standard variable tariffs with fluctuating prices, time-of-use (TOU) tariffs offer lower unit prices during off-peak hours - typically evenings and overnight - when your heat pump might be running the most. Many suppliers are now also starting to provide special rates for heat pump owners:

- Lower Off-Peak Rates: Powering your ASHP with cheaper electricity during off-peak hours can achieve significant savings. If your home is well insulated and your heat pump's control panel allows for scheduling, you can optimise your usage further. Set your heat pump to run without weather compensation at an increased flow temperature during the early hours to heat your home, then switch to weather compensation when TOU tariffs increase in the morning to maintain comfort levels. This strategy can save you a lot of money over the winter heating season.
- Cheap Night Time Electricity: If you have an immersion heater in your hot water cylinder, time-of-use tariffs with free or extremely cheap night-time electricity can be a game-changer for your energy bills. By scheduling your immersion heater to operate during these periods, you can heat your hot water for little to no cost. This reduces your reliance on daytime electricity, which is usually more expensive on TOU plans.

Finding Your Perfect Energy Match

Choosing the best energy plan for your heat pump requires some strategic thinking:
- Analyse Usage: Track your electricity consumption patterns to identify peak and off-peak periods. This will help you understand when your heat pump uses the most energy.
- Compare TOU Plans: Focus on plans with attractive off-peak rates that align with your heat pump's heating schedule and your daily routine.
- Fixed vs. Variable Rates: Decide between fixed or variable rates. Fixed rates offer predictability, while variable rates fluctuate with market conditions. Choose based on your risk tolerance and budget preferences.
- Government Grants: Explore financial incentives like the Smart Export Guarantee (SEG). This programme rewards you for exporting excess solar energy back to the grid.
- Smart Meter: To take advantage of TOU tariffs and maximise your savings, a smart meter is required. Smart meters automatically track your electricity consumption, allowing you to see exactly how much energy you're using during peak and off-peak periods. This data is key to analysing usage patterns and selecting the most cost-effective TOU plan for your home. If you don't have a smart meter, energy suppliers offer smart meter installations free of charge. Contact your electricity provider to discuss their smart meter options and how to get one installed in your home.

Lodging an Installation Complaint

If you're a new heat pump owner dealing with a poorly executed installation, remember that you have certain rights and options for recourse. However, it's important to approach this realistically. While the theoretical processes for resolution seem straightforward, they often fall short in practice.

Our experience assisting numerous homeowners with substandard installations has revealed significant inefficiencies within the complaints system. Organisations like MCS and consumer codes, which are designed to safeguard homeowners, frequently pass responsibilities among themselves without providing effective solutions. This bureaucratic shuffle not only tests homeowners' patience but also drains their energy, often leading to resignation. It's a disheartening reality in the industry that needs to be acknowledged and addressed.

Therefore, it's essential to take every precaution to ensure your heating system is installed correctly from the outset, avoiding the struggle of dealing with a poorly executed installation. But that's not always possible, so here's a streamlined guide to lodging a complaint:

Gather Evidence
- Contract and Documentation: Collect all paperwork related to the installation, including quotes, invoices, contracts, deliverables, warranties and emails.
- Photo and Video Record: Document any visible issues with the installation, such as poor workmanship, leaks or damage.
- Performance Monitoring: Track temperature readings, energy consumption and any significant performance discrepancies from promised efficiency.

Contact the Installer
- Initial Communication: Attempt to resolve the issue directly with the installer. Clearly communicate the problems you've encountered and request rectification.
- Follow-up in Writing: Keep a record of communications by sending emails or letters outlining the issues and proposed solutions.

Seek Third-Party Support
- MCS: If the installer is MCS-certified, their work is backed by a warranty scheme. Contact the MCS and lodge a complaint to initiate an investigation.
- Trading Standards: Trading Standards investigate unfair trading practices. If you suspect misrepresentation or poor workmanship, consider contacting them.
- Contact the consumer codes:
    - ✓ RECC: If your installer is RECC-certified, their independent dispute resolution service provides additional protection.
    - ✓ HIES: HIES members also offer a dedicated complaints procedure.
- Independent engineers: Hiring an independent engineer to assess the installation can provide professional validation of your concerns.

Legal Action
- Small Claims Court: For disputes under £30,000, consider using the Small Claims Court. Legal costs are lower, and you can represent yourself.
- Solicitors: In more complex cases, consult a solicitor specialising in construction or consumer law. They can advise on available legal options and represent you in court.

Glossary

Navigating heat pumps and their technical jargon can feel like deciphering a foreign language when you're starting out. This glossary equips you with a comprehensive understanding of common heat pump terminology, empowering you to make informed decisions and have productive conversations with engineers or service providers.

Air-Air Heat Pump: This type of heat pump captures heat from outdoor air using a fan. It then transfers this heat indoors, warming your space. Clever engineering allows it to also work in reverse, acting as an air conditioner to cool your home in warmer months.

Air-Water Heat Pump: This heat pump works similarly to the air-air version, but instead of distributing warm air directly, it heats water. This hot water can then be circulated throughout your home using radiators or underfloor heating to provide warmth. Some air-water heat pumps can even heat your domestic hot water supply for showers and taps.

Ambient Temperature: The surrounding air temperature.

Anti-Freeze: A solution added to the ASHP's water loop to prevent freezing during cold weather operation. Ethylene or propylene glycol is most commonly used in heat pump systems.

Anti-Freeze Valves: Some manufacturers require freeze protection for their units due to the type of pump installed, which cannot tolerate freezing conditions—this is common with most wet circulator pumps. To mitigate this issue, antifreeze valves are installed at the lowest point, typically on the heat pump. These valves open and discharge the system water when the pipe temperature approaches or reaches the freezing point, effectively removing it from the system to prevent freezing damage.

Bivalent Heat Pump System: A bivalent heat pump system teams up a heat pump with another heating source, like a boiler. This creates a more robust heating solution. The system relies on smart controls to decide which source is most efficient at any given time. This can depend on factors like outdoor temperature and heating demand.

Blending Valve: Merges two flows into one, adjusting the output temperature accordingly for either heating or cooling purposes. It regulates the delivery temperature based on specific requirements and is commonly used in underfloor heating valve packs to lower the system temperature and prevent floor overheating.

Buffer Tank: A storage tank that holds heated water from the ASHP, creating a thermal reserve and improving system efficiency by reducing short cycling (frequent on/off cycles).

By-pass Valve (DHW): A valve that diverts refrigerant flow to prioritise hot water heating when needed (relevant for ASHP models with DHW capabilities).

Coil: A heat exchanger with a series of tubes that absorbs or releases heat, depending on the refrigerant's state.

Condenser Coil (Outdoor Unit): Releases heat extracted from your home to the outside air.

Evaporator Coil (Indoor Unit): Absorbs heat from your indoor air.

Compressor: The heart of the ASHP system, responsible for compressing refrigerant to create the pressure differential required for heat transfer.

Condensate: The moisture removed from the air during cooling mode. This condensate is typically drained away from the system.

Coefficient of Performance (COP): A ratio that measures the efficiency of the ASHP in heating mode. It represents the amount of heat output (in BTUs) for every unit of electrical energy input (in watts). Higher COP indicates better efficiency.

Defrost Cycle: In cold weather, the outdoor unit might go into defrost mode to melt frost accumulated on the condenser coil, ensuring efficient heat exchange.

Diverting Valve: Redirects water from one port to another. It's commonly employed in heat pump and boiler systems that utilise hot water priority or a 'W' piping plan.

Delta T (ΔT): Refers to the difference between two temperatures, typically used to measure the temperature variation between two pipes, such as the flow and return lines in a heating system.

Domestic Hot Water (DHW): Refers to hot water used for showers, taps, and other household applications. Some ASHP models can be integrated with a hot water storage tank to provide DHW heating.

Energy Efficiency Ratio (EER): A ratio that measures the efficiency of the ASHP in cooling mode. It represents the amount of cooling output (in BTUs) for every unit of electrical energy input (in watts). Higher EER indicates better efficiency.

Fan Speed: Modern ASHPs often offer variable fan speeds, allowing for quieter operation or increased airflow depending on your needs.

Heat Exchanger: A component within the heat pump enables heat transfer between circuits without mixing them. The heat pump contains two heat exchangers: one for the hot side (the condenser) and the other for the cold side (the evaporator).

Heat Pump Rating: A heat pump is assigned a heat output rating, measured in kilowatts (kW), which can change based on the operating temperatures. The amount of electrical power it consumes to produce this heat typically ranges from 25% to 50% of the heat output value.

Humidity: The amount of water in the air, or relative humidity (RH), measured by a wet-dry thermometer based on evaporative cooling, directly correlates with temperature; for example, air at 80% RH at 2°C becomes approximately 21% RH at 20°C, indicating that as temperature increases, humidity decreases for the same water content, affecting comfort levels and the amount of energy needed for temperature adjustment.

Inverter Technology: Advanced ASHP models utilise inverter technology that allows the compressor to adjust its speed to match the heating or cooling demand, resulting in improved efficiency and quieter operation.

Kilowatt (kW): A unit of power equal to 1,000 watts. ASHP capacities are often measured in kilowatts (kW).

Kilowatt Hour (kWh): A unit of energy consumption equal to the amount of energy used by a 1 kW appliance running for one hour. Electricity bills are typically based on kWh consumption.

Legionella: A bacterium responsible for Legionnaires' disease and other Legionellosis illnesses, becomes active and can multiply between 20°C and 45°C, remains inactive below 20°C and between 45°C and 50°C, and is eliminated above 50°C, with higher temperatures killing it more rapidly. Inhaling vapour containing its spores is necessary for infection, and risks can be minimised by maintaining water temperatures outside its active range, primarily through pasteurisation or other temperature management strategies.

Load Compensation: is a heating control strategy that adjusts the heat output of a heating system based on the actual heating demand within a building. It monitors the indoor temperature and modulates the heat provided by the system to match the needs of the space.

MCS (Microgeneration Certification Scheme): A UK certification scheme that ensures heat pumps meet specific efficiency and safety standards. MCS-certified heat pumps are eligible for certain government grants and financial incentives.

Modulation: This describes a system where an electrical or mechanical device adjusts its power input or flow rate, or both, to consistently maintain a specific temperature or flow rate as set by the user.

Phase Change: The transformation of a substance from one state of matter to another – solid to liquid, liquid to gas, or vice versa. This process is crucial in the heating industry, especially for the operation of heat pumps, which use the vapour compression cycle, and for phase change energy storage systems.

Refrigerant: A special fluid that absorbs and releases heat as it changes state (liquid to gas and vice versa) within the ASHP system.

Refrigeration Cycle: The thermodynamic process by which the ASHP transfers heat from your home to the outdoors (cooling mode) or vice versa (heating mode).

Reverse Cycle Heat Pump: Refers to the ability of the ASHP to operate in both heating and cooling modes by reversing the direction of refrigerant flow.

Sensor: Electronic devices that measure various parameters like temperature or pressure within the ASHP system, providing feedback to the control board.

Short Cycling: Describes a heat pump's compressor rapidly switching on and off, typically running less than a few minutes per cycle.

Split System: The most common type of ASHP system consisting of two separate units: an indoor unit (air handler) and an outdoor unit (condenser).

Stratification: Stratification refers to the temperature difference within a water body, from top to bottom, caused by natural heat movement–warm water rises while cooler water sinks. This phenomenon is often observed in domestic water cylinders where water remains still. Here, the process of convection is at play: heat from the coil in the tank is absorbed by the water, which then moves upwards, leaving the water at the bottom cooler.

System Efficiency: The capability to achieve desired results or products with minimal effort, expense, or waste; a measure of effectiveness and resource optimisation.

System Separator: used in systems where the secondary flow rate exceeds the primary flow rate, originally developed for high-temperature, on-off boilers. It ensures adequate flow through the secondary circuit, which typically operates at a lower temperature than the primary circuit.

Thermostat: A programmable device that controls the operating temperature of the ASHP system and maintains your desired comfort level.

TRV: A Thermostatic Radiator Valve is a self-regulating valve fitted to radiators in heating systems. It controls the temperature of a room by adjusting the flow of hot water to the radiator based on the setting selected, helping to maintain the desired comfort level within the space.

Two Port Valve: Halts or diminishes the flow in a pipe and can be operated either manually or automatically.

Viscosity: Refers to how much a fluid (whether liquid or gas) resists flowing or changing shape when different parts of it move relative to each other. For example, syrup, being more viscous than water, flows less easily.

Volumiser: Aims to expand the system's volume, especially in fixed-output installations, to minimise cycling and extend operating times. It can be installed either on the flow or return side. When placed on the flow side, it captures high-temperature heat, which generally leads to longer run times for a given size.

Make Your Own Notes Here:

Units of Measurement

Pressure
- Bar: The basic unit of pressure.
- Metres of Head: 1 Bar is equivalent to 10 meters of head.
- Pascals (Pa): 1 Bar equals 1,000,000 Pascals.
- Kilopascals (kPa): 1 Bar is equal to 100 kPa.
- Megapascals (mPa): 1 Bar corresponds to 10 mPa.

Velocity
- Metres per Second (m/s): The standard unit for measuring velocity in fluid dynamics.
- Volume
- Cubic Metres (m^3): Used for measuring large volumes.
- Litres (L): 1 cubic meter is equivalent to 1000 litres.
- Millilitres (mL): 1 litre equals 1000 millilitres.

Flow
- Cubic Metres Per Hour (m^3/hr): Commonly used to measure flow rate in larger systems.
- Litres Per Minute (L/min): 1 cubic meter per hour translates to approximately 16.66 litres per minute.
- Litres per Second (L/sec): 1 cubic meter per hour is equal to about 0.28 litres per second.

Make Your Own Notes Here:

Make Your Own Notes Here:

Printed in Great Britain
by Amazon